Praise for Th

How different would the world be if every human being developed the practice of resting in their belovedness? This book was written by a man who has lived these practices and seen the fruit in his life and relationship with the Lord. This book is a gift to the church! It is a practical, guided path for the follower of Jesus desiring to cultivate lasting intimacy with God.

—Jay Pathak, National Director of Vineyard USA and coauthor of *The Art of Neighboring: Building Genuine Relationships Right Outside Your Door*

In *The Intimate God*, Alan Kraft takes us through essential truths that help us grow as students of Jesus. He beautifully explains and illustrates God's delight for us, which is ground zero in discipleship, and then leads us in practices to help imprint this important concept on our souls. I recommend you not only read this book but grab some friends and go through the practices together. You will see each other transform before your eyes.

—Michel Hendricks, Director of Life Model Consulting and coauthor of *The Other Half of Church: Christian Community, Brain Science, and Overcoming Spiritual Stagnation*

This book is a practical and biblical guide to living with Jesus more abundantly. It is an invitation to the intimate relationship God designed but so many Christians miss out on. Pastor Alan leads us to delight and abide in Jesus throughout our day in a way that is simple and practical yet life changing. If you feel like you know about Jesus but don't know Him and experience Him like you desire, then this is the book for you.

—Lyndsey Oates, Head Volleyball Coach,
University of Northern Colorado

While doctrine alone can make us feel stuck, practicing the great truths of Jesus' ways and teachings offers us real life and freedom. Alan Kraft offers us an "easy to do and easy to get" practice manual of the inner life of the kingdom. I highly commend this resource for your personal journey or to journey together as a group!

—Stephen W. Smith, author of *The Lazarus Life: Spiritual Transformation for Ordinary People* and *Soul Custody: Choosing to Care for the One and Only You*

I've known Alan Kraft for years and appreciate his heart for deepening his personal walk of faith and helping others do the same. In his latest book, *The Intimate God*, he guides readers through a seven-week interactive study aimed at a growing intimacy with God. I found his practical suggestions helpful as I seek intentional time and space for growing my awareness of Jesus' presence in every aspect of my life.

—Kevin Kompelien, President,
Evangelical Free Church of America

True followers of Jesus aspire to a faith that is genuine and transformational. Unfortunately, for many a profession of faith does not translate into an intimate life of faith with God. Alan Kraft has provided a fresh, practical guide which is at once simple and profound toward engaging the mind and awakening the heart. Read it. Practice it. And experience the love and presence of God.

—Tom Shirk, Senior Pastor, Calvary Bible Church, Boulder, Colorado

Pursuing intimacy with God is what we have been made for! Alan's insights into how we can more effectively pursue this intimacy are refreshing. The practices in this book will help you establish doable rhythms in your daily life to deepen your relationship with Jesus. This is one resource you will use instead of putting it on your bookshelf to collect dust.

—Barry Vegter, District Superintendent, Evangelical Free Church of America, Rocky Mountain District

Alan has provided a fresh invitation to further pursue Jesus. Intimacy is within our reach, and this packing list for the journey includes timeless disciplines and helpful directives to spur us on. This resource is a great road map for individuals or for a group experience.

—Mark Hoffman, Lead Pastor, Two Rivers Church, Knoxville, Tennessee

A 7-WEEK JOURNEY

THE
INTIMATE
GOD

A Practical Guide to Experiencing
the God Who Delights in You

ALAN KRAFT

ILLUMIFY
MEDIA.COM

Published by
Illumify Media Global
www.IllumifyMedia.com
"Let's bring your book to life!"

Paperback ISBN: 978-1-959099-42-0

Typeset by Art Innovations (http://artinnovations.in/)
Cover design by Debbie Lewis

Printed in the United States of America

To my amazing wife and children who so powerfully embody for me the love of Jesus.

Contents

Acknowledgments

A special thanks to Steve Oeffling and Stetson Beaman for their valuable input during those Zoom calls in COVID isolation; to my daughter Erin who read every word and offered incredibly helpful and practical input; to Nate Davis who offered helpful suggestions through the book; to the staff team at Christ Community who willingly experienced and practiced this material together; and finally, to the amazing people at Christ Community who are journeying with me in what it means to abide in the love and life of Jesus.

Introduction

I'm guessing you are reading this book because you long for something more in your relationship with Jesus.

I can relate.

For the first twenty years of my Christian life, I sincerely wanted to know Jesus intimately. I longed to enjoy an experiential closeness with Him. Being a pastor, I knew that the Bible described that kind of experience as being normal for a Christian. But it wasn't a part of my life.

My "experience" with Jesus felt distant, disciplined, and impersonal. It wasn't that I didn't love Jesus or that I didn't want to know Him better. But the path I was on didn't seem to be moving me toward a deepening *intimacy* with Jesus. Honestly, that word wasn't even on my spiritual radar. And that was part of the problem. I had settled for a relationship with Jesus that avoided intimacy with Jesus.

Intimacy speaks of a depth of closeness to another person that requires vulnerability. Being known. No hiding. No pretending. Letting ourselves be seen and known for who we really are, not who we think we're supposed to be.

Intimacy = into-me-see.

That's the kind of relationship our intimate God longs to have with us, but I'm not sure I *functionally* believed that. I believed it theologically . . . but it wasn't a part of my experience. How often did I miss seeing His true heart?

A number of years ago, in the midst of a season of burn-out, I found my way to a soul care retreat center located in the mountains. After my morning session with my spiritual director, he left the property, so I had the place all to myself. I made my way to a nearby hammock, trying to find the rest that my depleted soul so desperately needed.

After briefly falling asleep, I woke up and immediately saw a huge thunderhead being formed right before my eyes. For as long as I can remember, I have loved watching thunderheads build in the sky, but never had I been so close to the action. From my front row seat, I watched with awe this roiling cloud get shaped. After several minutes of utter enjoyment, I had this thought: *God, did You do that just for me? Did You orchestrate that to remind my weary soul that You see me and know me?*

That thought filled my heart with wonder. What if this inti-mate God was revealing His heart to me more than I realized? What if I began to intentionally cultivate spaces and moments to experience Him more deeply?

That's what this book is about.

Practicing Intimacy

Over the course of my own journey, I have discovered some practical ways we can intentionally create space in our lives to more deeply experience our intimate God. I can't wait to share these things with you. In many ways, this book is a practical field guide for how you can grow in your experience of intimacy with Jesus.

Let me say that again. This book is a *practical* field guide. In other words, this book is about *doing* stuff. Not just thinking about or memorizing or discussing concepts and ideas. This guidebook is about doing. It's about practicing. It's about experiencing.

Which means that if you have picked up this resource hoping for a quick read that can immediately result in a deeper experience with Jesus, feel free to return this book to Amazon. That's not what this resource is about. It is not intended to simply be read.

This book focuses on learning about certain truths and then actually taking the time to *practice* those truths. Call it "homework" . . . or maybe not. Let's stick to the "practice" word.

But what kind of practice are we talking about? We've all heard the phrase "Practice makes perfect." Not true. The truth is, practice makes *permanent*. What we practice becomes a part of our lives for a long time.

Which brings up an unsettling reality—we are all practicing something. We all are practicing a way of living that either establishes spiritual realities more deeply in our lives or cultivates other realities. There really is no middle-ground, passive approach to spirituality. You *are* being spiritually formed. The crucial question is, By what?

I recently heard author and pastor John Mark Comer describe how each of us is on one of two spiritual formation pathways. He describes one as "unintentional spiritual formation."[1]

Unintentional spiritual formation occurs when we are doing life with no intentionality regarding the path we are on. The movies we watch, the books we read, the conversations we have, the podcasts we listen to, the people we follow on social media, the friends we hang out with, etc. are shaping our spirituality without us realizing it. They actively shape the way we feel about ourselves, the way we think about God, as well as the way we view other people.

We *are* being shaped in a particular direction. But it is unintentional—which is kind of scary. It's happening and we are letting it happen, but we aren't intentionally directing or steering that trajectory toward what our heart longs for—a deeper closeness to Jesus.

The obvious alternative to this pathway is *intentional* spiritual formation, where we take ownership of the path we are on. We choose to build into the rhythm of our lives practices that help us experience Jesus more deeply.

That's what this field guide is intended to do. It is designed to help you build into your life specific practices that over time will help you grow in your experience of intimacy with Jesus.

In Matthew 7, Jesus concluded His well-known Sermon on the Mount by describing one person who built their house on the rock and another who built their house on the sand. When a storm inevitably came, the house on the sand collapsed while the one built on the rock stood firm. What made the difference?

"Therefore everyone who hears these words of mine and *puts them into practice* is like a wise man who built his house on the rock" (Matthew 7:24, emphasis mine).

There's that word again. *Practice.*

This book is designed as a seven-week journey that includes both content as well as opportunities to experience what you are learning. At the end of each week's content, there will be a few exercises for you to do that week to apply the content from that chapter. These exercises are not optional. They are essential.

Intimacy with Jesus cannot be experienced by simply reading a book. It is something to be *experienced* through practice. Most of the exercises can be done in ten to fifteen minutes. I recommend spreading out the exercises throughout your week, rather than trying to do them all at once.

Over the course of the content and exercises in the next seven weeks, you will be introduced to five easily accessible spiritual practices that have helped me experience a deeper connection with Jesus and can do the same for you. The seven-week structure is only a recommendation. Feel free to slow down at any point, spending more than one week in any chapter. The goal is not *getting through* the content. The goal is *experiencing* the content.

Journeying with Others

While the content and exercises are designed for you to experience by yourself, feel free to invite some friends or a small group to take this journey alongside you. The process of learning new spiritual practices is often significantly enhanced when we pursue this together with others and can share honestly how the journey is going—the joys as well as the struggles.

In the appendix of this book, there are some suggested small group questions to help facilitate this kind of group experience.

Are You Ready?

Today marks the beginning of a lifelong journey. But before we begin this journey, let's stop and remember the goal.

Intimacy with Jesus.

These exercises and practices are simply a means to that end. This is not about checking off boxes. It's about relationship. Jesus invites you into a deeper relationship with Him.

My prayer is that Jesus uses this resource to help make that happen in your life.

You ready? Let's get practicing!

WEEK ONE

How Does God Feel About You?

How does God feel about you?

Actually, let me rephrase that. How do you *feel* God feels about you? I'm not interested in the Sunday school answer: "God loves me." We all know that, at some level. We know the right answer. My question is, How fully are you *experiencing* that reality?

How you answer that question has a huge impact on your experience of intimacy with Jesus.

Think about this analogy: Imagine that you are back in the fourth grade. Your teacher is a stern, stoic, older woman who never smiles and who always has a disappointed look on her face. Every assignment you turn in gets returned with lots of corrections. She freely dispenses punishments for even minor misbehaviors.

Your parents rave about what a great teacher she is. She has various teaching awards on the walls of her classroom. You learn things in her class, but you never feel relaxed in her classroom.

Let's say that one day she comes to you as the bell rings and says, "I'd like to help tutor you in astronomy. I know that is an interest of yours. And I'd love to get to know you better and hear more about your family and your other interests. Would you like to come by after school on Tuesdays?"

What would your internal response be? *No way. I am not doing that.* Even though you respect this person and could probably learn something from her, you don't want to get to know her. She intimidates you. You're afraid of her. Nothing you do is ever enough.

Your perception of her impacts your desire to get to know her better.

Now think about how this relates to our perception of God. If we perceive God to be distant, uncaring, and distracted, or that He wears a continual scowl on His face, how eager will we be to spend time with Him? We won't. No matter how often we are told that Christians are *supposed* to spend time with God, we won't *want* to spend time with Him.

And when we do force ourselves to spend time with Him, how safe will we feel being real about what's going on in our life? We won't. If we don't feel His love and acceptance, we will instinctively keep our guard up. The result? A distant, emotionally disengaged relationship rather than the intimate relationship we long for.

Our experience of intimacy with Jesus is completely dependent upon our perception of Him, which means that we desperately need an accurate perception in our minds and hearts of how He feels about us.

Being Delighted In

At the heart of Christianity is this amazing gospel reality: God delights in you. Seriously. It's not just that He tolerates you or that He reluctantly accepts you. God *actually* delights in you. This delight is the starting place for our relational connection as human beings.

Our son and daughter-in-law recently had a beautiful baby boy named Silas. How we love that little guy! During a recent visit, we spent hours getting Silas to smile. How? By delighting in him. Anytime we would smile at him, his face would light up (and light up our hearts as well). It never got old, to him or to us.

This is how God made us as human beings. Neuroscience reveals that when a child sees the face of someone delighting in them, two things happen in that child's brain: joy is released and a relational attachment occurs.[2] Every human being is created with a need, a longing, to be delighted in. When that happens, a door opens for relational connection and intimacy.

If you walk into a room and someone you know looks up at you with no response and then goes back to working on their computer, how connected do you feel to them? But what if they smile at you the moment they look up and see you? You feel an immediate attachment to them. (Just try this in your relationships and see how people respond.)

In light of this relational impact of delight, it is no surprise to discover that this language of delight is often how our intimate God describes His heart toward us.

For the LORD your God is living among you.
He is a mighty savior.
He will take delight in you with gladness.
With his love, he will calm all your fears.
He will rejoice over you with joyful songs. (Zephaniah 3:17 NLT)

9

The image portrayed is that of a loving parent, tenderly holding a fitful baby, calming their infant's restlessness by singing with joy over this child in their arms. That is God's heart for you. God delights in you. He rejoices over you. This is how He sincerely feels about you.

Or how about in Numbers 6, where God gives the priests a specific blessing to speak continually over the people as a reflection of what God wants them to experience: "Say to them: 'The LORD bless you and keep you; the LORD make his face shine on you and be gracious to you; the LORD turn his face toward you and give you peace.' So they will put my name on the Israelites, and I will bless them" (Numbers 6:23–27).

Notice how twice in this passage God's face is mentioned. *May His face shine on you*—that literally means He's smiling at you. A genuine smile of delight. And secondly, this passage describes the Lord's face being turned *toward* you—not turned away or distracted on his cell phone. His heart is turned toward you.

Imagine the impact in your everyday life if you regularly experienced the Lord delighting in you rather than you feeling His disappointment or distance. What would that do to your desire for deeper intimacy with Him? This is an absolute game-changer.

An Experiential Resource

Thankfully, God has given us a specific resource to help us *experience* His lavish love for us and delight in us. Check out what Paul says in Romans 5:5. "God's love has been poured out into our hearts through the Holy Spirit, who has been given to us."

The language Paul uses is not describing a trickle. This is Niagara Falls. God's love is being lavishly, abundantly poured out. Where? "Into our hearts," Paul says. From a biblical perspective, the heart is the central location of our passions, our desires, and our emotions. Paul is talking about an *experience* of God's love. Something we *feel* at the core of our being.

Now, I realize this "feelings" stuff may be making some of you nervous. Early in my Christian life, I was taught that I shouldn't expect to feel God's love for me. Feelings are too suspicious and unreliable. I just needed to make sure I knew the truth in my head. That perspective kept me from experiencing intimacy with Jesus for many years.[3]

But Paul totally expected us to continually experience (i.e., feel) the Niagara Falls of God's love being poured out into our hearts. So how does this experience happen? Paul tells us in this same verse: it's "through the Holy Spirit, who has been given to us" (Romans 5:5).

The Holy Spirit has been given to us by God to help you and me experience the fullness of Jesus' love for us. So, what does this look like practically speaking? Paul describes this a bit later in the book of Romans: "The Spirit you received does not make you slaves, so that you live in fear again; rather, the Spirit you received brought about your adoption to sonship. And by him we cry, 'Abba, Father.' The Spirit himself testifies with our spirit that we are God's children" (Romans 8:15–16).

Notice how actively the Spirit in us is working to help us experience the fullness of God's love. Not only has He brought about our adoption as fully loved and accepted sons and daughters of God; He also continually stirs within us a powerful longing for intimate connection with God. Look again at verse 15: "And by him we cry, 'Abba, Father.'"

The word *Abba* is what a child would call his or her dad. In today's terminology it means "Daddy" or "Papa." Paul is saying that the Spirit is continually stirring in us a cry, a longing, to feel God's tender and fatherly love and delight in us.

But there's more.

Paul also says here that this Spirit within us "testifies with our spirit that we are children of God" (Romans 8:16). Think about that. To testify means to speak the truth. The Spirit within us is continually communicating to our inner being, our heart, a very specific truth: that we are a beloved child of God.

In other words, the Spirit within you is continually whispering to your heart, *"You are my son whom I love. You are my daughter whom I adore. With you, I am well pleased."*

Amazing.

The intimate God so wants you to experience intimacy with Him that He has placed within you His Spirit, whose primary job description is to continually remind you of that love.

This is the journey we are beginning—learning how to tune in to the Spirit's presence within us so that we actually feel how much He loves us.

The exercises and practices in the rest of this book are designed to help you grow in this beautiful, transformative experience.

Whole-Brained Spirituality

I want to introduce you to a practical tool that has helped me better hear the Spirit's whisper and grow in my experience of Jesus' love for me.

Over the past two to three decades, amazing progress has been made in understanding how our brains process information. At the risk of oversimplification, the left side of our brain tends to focus on data, facts, and content—what we typically refer to as the mind.

This side of our brain embraces truth cognitively and propositionally. This is the realm of algebra, of science, of theological study. The biblical idea of God's holiness, for instance, is an objective truth our mind needs to understand and embrace.

The right side of our brain is the intuitive, relational side—where we experience emotions, attachment, as well as our identity. In a nutshell, the right side of our brain is the experiential center— the heart, if you will. This explains why, for many people, listening to or singing a worship song can be so powerful. It touches their hearts in an experiential way by activating the right side of their brain.

Both sides of our brain are created by God and vitally important to utilize. However, most of us tend to lean heavily—even exclusively—on the left side of our brain when it comes to our relationship with God: sermons, seminars, books, content, and information.

This explains how I was able to graduate with a master's degree in theology and yet in my heart not really feel God's love for me. Information about God's love didn't result in me experiencing that love. Something was missing.

That "something" was me learning how also to engage the right side of my brain—the experiential part of me—so that the information I knew in my head became more real in my experience.

Biblical Imaging

One of the "right brain" tools that has helped me experience God's love for me is what I refer to as biblical imaging. In biblical imaging, we take a truth articulated in Scripture, and we let the right side of our brain envision it happening. In other words, we use our God-given imagination to picture the scriptural truth in our minds.

For most of us, our brains instinctively and often picture things in this way. When I think of my wife, Raylene, I don't see a paragraph with words. I see an image, a picture of her in my mind . . . and that image touches my emotions. It makes my relationship with her more real in this moment.

Think about the power of this in our spiritual lives. If we take a truth that is already in the informational (left) side of our brain and we intentionally engage the experiential (right) side of our brain by envisioning or imaging it in our minds, we *experience* that truth more deeply. It becomes more real to us.

This practice of biblical imaging is seen throughout Scripture. One of the most powerful examples is found in Psalm 27, where David, in the midst of some fear-inducing circumstances, chooses a particular response: "One thing I ask from the LORD, this only do I seek: that I may dwell in the house of the LORD all the days of my life, to gaze on the beauty of the LORD and to seek him in his temple" (Psalm 27:4).

The Hebrew word used here for "gaze" refers not to physical sight but to "seeing" in the spiritual realm—like a prophet "seeing" a vision. David intentionally uses his imagination to envision in his mind the beauty of the Lord. In doing so, David more deeply experiences the truth of God's beauty.

What we envision, we experience.

We see this principle at work in various areas of life. In professional sports like golf and basketball, athletes train to mentally "see" a shot before hitting it. When we remember a pleasant memory from our past, our brain experiences that memory as if it is happening again. What we envision, we experience.

Scripture is filled with examples of this. We are encouraged to "[fix] our eyes on Jesus" (Hebrews 12:2), to "set [our] minds on things above" (Colossians 3:2), and to "contemplate the Lord's glory" (2 Corinthians 3:18). These passages make no sense unless they refer to realities we envision in our minds.

In biblical imaging, we simply take a truth found in Scripture, and we allow the right side of our brain to envision or to picture that truth.[4] In doing so, we experience more deeply the truths contained in Scripture.

For me personally, this practice of biblical imaging has dramatically impacted my experience of Jesus' love for me. It has deepened my experience of intimacy with Him.

Practicing This Reality

I want to lead you in a spiritual exercise of biblical imaging that has been pivotal for me in helping me experience an accurate perception of God truly delighting in me—especially after I've failed or when I feel distant from Him.

I know this may be a bit out of your comfort zone. That's okay. This is how we learn. Even if it feels different or awkward, keep at it. I think you will find it to be extremely helpful.

Let's begin by quieting our hearts. Take a few deep breaths. Make sure all electronic devices around you are turned off. We want an environment with no distractions.

In this exercise, we are going to place ourselves in the story of the prodigal son, which Jesus describes in Luke 15. In this story, Jesus tells about a father who had two sons. One day, the younger son demanded his share of the estate—which was a huge insult to his dad. He was basically saying to his dad, "You are better off to me dead. I only want your money."

So, the father gave him his half of the estate. The younger son then left and squandered the entire amount on wild living. He lost everything. The only job he could find in his state of desperation was feeding pigs. He was so hungry that the pig food started to look good to him.

At that moment, Jesus says, he came to his senses. He decided to go back to his father and ask if he could work for him as a hired hand.

So now I want you to engage the right side of your brain by imagining yourself in this story. Take your time in this story.

Don't hurry this.

Picture in your mind yourself walking toward home, after having blown it big-time. You've got your speech prepared for your father—*Father, I am not even worthy to be called your son. Could I work as an employee?*

Can you see this in your mind?

As you walk this path that is getting nearer to your home, you have no idea how your heavenly Father will react to seeing you. You insulted Him horribly. You rejected Him. How will He now respond when He sees you? Take a moment and imagine that feeling.

Now as you walk over a small hill, suddenly your house is in view. Picture it in your mind.

You notice that your Father is on the back porch. He is looking for you to return. When He sees you, He pulls up His robe and begins running toward you. Envision the Father doing this.

As He gets close to you, you begin your prepared speech about not being worthy to be His son or daughter, but He's not listening. His face is filled with delight in seeing you. He wraps His arms around you and gives you a huge bear hug. Imagine this in your mind. Feel Him doing this with you.

He then holds your face in His hands and smiles with delight. Let Him delight in you.

Now picture Him taking His family robe and putting it across your shoulders. Feel the warmth and security of that.

He looks at your worn-out sandals and says to his servants, "Get my child some new Birkenstocks." And He gently places them on your weary feet. Completely undeserved. Feel His loving provision for you.

Now picture Him taking a family ring and putting it on your finger. Imagine Him saying to you, "You belong in this family. You are My son, My daughter. I am so glad to see you. You are Mine. Let's go celebrate."

Envision Him placing His arm around you as you walk back home together. How does that feel? Take a moment and enjoy Him being with you and loving you.

———

Let's debrief that experience. I realize this may have been a very new experience for you. It may have felt a little weird. That's okay. We're often not used to engaging our right brain in spiritual things, so at first it may feel a bit strange. That's normal.

Remember, the right side of our brain is the experiential side, where we feel emotions. This is why I encouraged you to stop periodically and ask, *How am I feeling in this moment?* Or another way to ask this is, *How is the truth of this Scripture impacting my heart right now?*

That's what we are after. This is not about exalting feelings over truth. This is about allowing biblical truth to touch our hearts.

Now, some of you may have gotten stuck in a particular part of the story. Maybe you couldn't envision the Father wrapping His arms of love around you. Maybe you could only envision Him standing in front of you. That's okay. God may be revealing something that He wants to explore further with you. This week in the exercises, you will have an opportunity to envision this passage again, and you can ask Him, *Why did I get stuck in this place?*

A friend of mine was doing this exercise and found that he couldn't experience the Father's embrace. So he later asked the Lord why that was, and God brought to his mind a memory of abuse in his past. As he welcomed the Lord's love into that pain, my friend was able to forgive the person who hurt him. When he then went back to Luke 15 in his imagination, he was able to feel the Father wrapping His arms around him. With tears in his eyes, he told me how impactful this experience had been for him.

If there are places like this where you feel stuck in this exercise, feel free to reach out to a counselor or someone who is proficient in the ministry of inner healing prayer.[5]

Next Steps

Having an accurate perception of God is foundational to your journey of experiencing deeper intimacy with God. This week's exercises are designed to help you experience more deeply the reality of a God who delights in you.

As explained in the introduction, each week's exercises are a crucial part of this journey. Content without practice has little impact. So don't skip the exercises. In fact, slow down in them. Take your time. Let the Lord pour out His love into your heart through His Spirit.

If you already have a devotional experience that is working for you, don't stop that. Simply find additional time throughout your week to do each week's exercises.

Exercises

EXERCISE ONE

In this exercise, I want you to place yourself again in the Luke 15 story as the prodigal son. Regularly doing this exercise can help you grow in experiencing the Father's love for you.

Find a quiet place where you can be alone with Jesus. Slowly read Luke 15:11–24.

Now place yourself back into the scene where you, as the prodigal son, are returning to your Father. Slowly envision yourself in each part of this story. Envision the Father running toward you, wrapping His arms around you, putting a robe on you, etc.

If you get stuck somewhere in the story, take some time to ask Jesus about that. *Why am I stuck here?* If He brings something to mind, invite Him into that situation and follow His guidance.

As you conclude this exercise, stay in this place for a few minutes, letting the Father love you. How does this feel? Enjoy His love for you.

EXERCISE TWO

Find a quiet place where you can be alone with Jesus.

In the story from Luke 15, there was another son in the family—the obedient son, who stayed home and did everything the father asked.

Slowly read the rest of the passage, Luke 15:25–32, and then answer the following questions.

- How would you describe the older brother's perception of his father? Is that perception accurate?
- How does the older brother's misperception impact him?
- How would you describe the older brother's identity?
- How does he view himself in relation to his father?

Now place yourself in this part of the story and envision yourself as the older brother. Play the scene out in your mind. What does the Father want to say to you? Where might you be missing out on an experience of the Father's love and why?

Take a minute and simply enjoy the Lord's love for you.

EXERCISE THREE

Find a quiet place where you can be alone with Jesus.

Slowly read the following paraphrase of Romans 8:15–16, where we have replaced "you" with either "I," "me," or "my": *The Spirit I received does not make me a slave, so that I live in fear again; rather, the Spirit I received brought about my adoption to sonship. And by him I cry, "Abba, Father." The Spirit himself testifies with my spirit that I am God's child.*

Slowly read it again. What stands out to you as you do so?

Is there any part of this passage that feels difficult for you to fully experience? Why is that?

Ask the Holy Spirit to deepen your experience of God as your "Abba" (*Abba* means "Papa" or "Daddy").

Ask the Holy Spirit to testify with your spirit that you are God's child. What do you hear Him say to you?

Take a moment to envision from Numbers 6:24–26 God's face being turned toward you and Him delighting in you. How does it feel to know He is smiling over you?

Recommended Resources for Further Exploration

Seeing Is Believing: Experiencing Jesus through Imaginative Prayer by Greg Boyd.

The Other Half of Church: Christian Community, Brain Science and Overcoming Spiritual Stagnation by Michel Hendricks

WEEK TWO

Stillness

Pause to Review

Take a moment to reflect on the following questions:

- How was your experience of the Father's love this past week?

- What was it like to imagine yourself in the prodigal son story?

I wish I could sit down with you over a cup of coffee and hear your experience of the exercises from last chapter. Those exercises are intended to provide an opportunity for you to begin to wade into a deeper experience of the God who absolutely delights in you!

This Week

Wouldn't it be amazing if we could build into our lives some regular practices that could enable us to drink more deeply of Jesus' love and delight in us? That is exactly what the rest of this book is about. You will begin building into your life some core spiritual practices that for centuries have helped believers in Jesus experience the depth of His presence and love.

This week we will focus on the spiritual practice of stillness, creating space in our lives to be still before the Lord.

Why Stillness?

Before I describe this practice in more detail, I want us to understand the why behind it. Why is the practice of stillness so important in our relationship with God?

The answer to that question is found all the way back in the first few chapters of Genesis. God creates Adam and Eve and places them in a beautiful garden. In this context, God delights in them and they in Him. It is this amazing picture of relational joy and shalom.

Everything in its right place.

Unfortunately, all of this blew up when Adam and Eve rebelled against God and because of their sin, they hid from His presence. For the first time ever, human beings experienced shame. They suddenly realized they were naked, and they felt exposed, dirty, unacceptable. So they hid from the face of God. We've been hiding ever since.

Even though God delights in us and longs for us to live in this constant love relationship with Him, we instinctively resist going there. We hide behind a wall of busyness, distraction, or even religious activity. Just like Adam and Eve, our feelings of being unacceptable and unworthy keep us from enjoying God's presence.

But notice in this story how God responds to Adam and Eve hiding in their shame: He moves *toward* them. You read that right. God actually moves toward Adam and Eve, and He asks them a very important question: "But the LORD God called to the man, 'Where are you?'" (Genesis 3:9).

Think about that. Why would God ask this question? It's not like He didn't know where they were. I mean, He's God. He knew exactly where they were. This was a not a geographical question. This was a relational question.

God was inviting them out of their hiding and into His presence. In asking this question, God reveals that He wants to meet them right where they are. But in order to do that, they must *admit* where they are. They must come out of hiding and admit their shame and brokenness.

The same thing is true of us. God continually asks us this same question: *"Where are you?"* Not the pretend you. Not the "trying hard to look like you have it all together" you. Not the busy, distracted you, or the stoic you who keeps stuffing your sadness or disappointment.

No. God wants the real you—the you who is filled with fear, the you who is overwhelmed with stress, the you who hasn't slept well for a week. God wants to meet you where you are, not where you think you are supposed to be. (You might want to read that last line again . . . it is super important.)

So, in light of this amazing truth, when do we ever slow down long enough to honestly answer the questions, *Where am I? Where is my heart right now? What thoughts are filling my mind? What is the condition of my soul?*

I recently came across a quote from a pastor in the seventeenth century who totally nailed our current reality: "There are some men and women who have lived forty or fifty years in the world and have had scarcely one hour's discourse with their hearts all the while."[6] Ouch.

When do we ever stop long enough to explore what our heart is experiencing?

We're often too busy, hurrying from one thing to the next, plodding through life, ignoring our heart. Then when we finally get some downtime, we fill it with Netflix or a game app on our phone, or social media or some other substance, activity, or dopamine hit that provides a temporary distraction, so that we don't have to look within and perhaps face our shame, our pain, our fears, and insecurities.

Even though we have an intimate God who continually turns His face toward us and who longs to pour His love into those vulnerable places, we often choose to live apart from that reality. So how do we fix this? Through the practice of stillness.

What Is Stillness?

Believers in Jesus have been engaging in this practice for centuries. In the practice of stillness, we intentionally create space in our lives to connect with our real selves—to slow down long enough so that we can answer God's question to us: *"Where are you . . . really?"*

And here's what makes stillness so powerful. When we slow down long enough to be present to ourselves in that moment, our souls become more attentive to the loving presence of God.

There is a powerful example of this in the Old Testament. In 1 Kings 18 we read about how Elijah, after a huge spiritual victory over the prophets of Baal, hears that King Ahab's wife is livid with rage and threatening to kill Elijah. Suddenly Elijah's inner world is turned upside down, and he finds himself in an emotionally dark place. "Elijah was afraid and ran for his life" (1 Kings 19:3).

Where does he go in this place of emotional despair and exhaustion? Elijah goes into a wilderness—a solitary place—and he opens his heart to God. He basically says, *I've had enough, God. Take my life. I'm a nobody.* Elijah is answering this question: *Where are you?* He is tuning in to his heart and acknowledging his fear, his insecurity, his discouragement.

And God meets him in that place.

When we don't take time for stillness, we end up disconnecting from our true selves, which hinders our ability to experience intimacy with Jesus. Remember the definition of intimacy? Into-me-see. If we are not aware of what is really going on inside us, how can we experience Jesus in that place?

The practice of stillness enables us to experience Jesus where we truly are, not where we think we are supposed to be.

Creating Space

So, how do we practice stillness? In my experience, there are three crucial aspects of this. First, we must *create space* for it. In Mark 1, we are told about how, after a day filled with teaching in a synagogue and healing people, the whole town gathered at Jesus' door that evening to receive even more from Him.

He was exhausted physically, spiritually, emotionally—which makes this next verse so powerful: "Very early in the morning, while it was still dark, Jesus got up, left the house and went off to a solitary place, where he prayed" (Mark 1:35).

Why would He do this? Why not sleep in? It's because He knew He needed this. His soul needed this, so He created space for this in His life.

For one thing, He created space in His *schedule* for stillness. He gets up early—while it was still dark. We need to carve out time for stillness. It won't happen automatically. It could be morning. It could be evening. It could be during the day. I find that morning works best for me, but you might struggle to focus in the morning, so you need to find another time that works. The key is building this into the rhythm of our lives so that it happens consistently. We carve out time in our schedule.

The other intentional "creating space" decision Jesus makes is to create space in his *environment* for stillness. Jesus goes to a solitary place. He goes to a place where he can be alone: no people, no distractions. We need to find a physical place for stillness. Probably not in a coffee shop with earbuds in or on our sofa with the television on. Stillness best occurs in a place where our usual distractions are removed.

This includes silencing our phone or putting it away somewhere so you can't see the notifications you are receiving. Or better yet, turning it off. (I know, crazy idea.) Our phones actually do have a "power off" button. We just rarely use it. One of the advantages of having one device that connects us to the whole world and everyone in it is that by shutting it off, we disconnect ourselves from the whole world and everyone in it.

Like Jesus, we must create a solitary place where we can retreat from the noise and distractions of the world. I know this can be challenging depending on your stage of life—especially if you have young children. In those seasons, your experience of stillness may only be for a couple of minutes behind a locked bathroom door. That's okay. Your soul needs this, even if it can only be for a few minutes.

Now, let me warn you. If you are not used to doing this, your initial experience of practicing stillness may be a bit unsettling. We are so used to hurry, constant noise, and activity that it can be a tad unnerving to stop and just be quiet. Our mind may start racing. We may start to feel a bit panicky. All of which are normal responses. A car driving at eighty miles per hour is not able to stop immediately on a dime.

The good news is that with practice you will get better at stillness. And you will find that your soul looks forward to this oasis from the busyness of life.

So, the first key to the practice of stillness is creating space: creating space in our schedule and space in an undistracted environment.

Being Present to Yourself

The second aspect to experiencing stillness is *being present to yourself*. In being present to myself, I slow down long enough to tune in to my inner being. I choose to pay attention to those parts of me that my busyness, distractions, and shame have kept me from exploring.

Like Elijah, we slow down long enough to answer that question that God is asking: *"Where are you right now?"* In slowing down for stillness, Elijah connected with those very real but neglected parts of himself that were feeling exhausted, discouraged, and afraid.

One of the biggest "aha" moments for me in this stillness journey occurred when I realized that I have many parts within me that comprise who I am. At any given moment, I am not simply experiencing one thought or one emotion. I have multiple thoughts and emotions.

I may be feeling excitement about a conversation the day before but also feeling nervous about a meeting coming up that morning. Part of me may be trying to figure out a solution to a situation at work, while another part of me is filled with joy at the most recent pictures of my grandson.

This is how God made us. Our inner being is a beautiful, complex, essential aspect of who we are. These various parts of us make up what many have referred to as our true self. I love that. My true self is who I really am, not the false image I'm trying to project to the world around me.

As I mentioned earlier, our struggle is that, due to busyness or distractions, we often don't give much attention to these parts of us; some are ignored entirely. This results in what author Chuck DeGroat refers to as "our scattered selves,"[7] which inevitably leads to fragmented lives.

Being present to ourselves through the practice of stillness provides a powerful antidote to this scattered reality. To use an analogy, in stillness we are inviting all the parts of us to the table. Every part is seen; every part has a voice.

Here's what this looks like for me. Once I've created space to be alone with God, I like to begin with some deep breaths to intentionally quiet my soul. Sometimes I attach a whispered prayer to the inhale and exhale. "Spirit of God" (inhale), "breathe on me" (exhale), or "Abba, Father" (inhale), "I belong to You" (exhale). This is often referred to as "spiritual breathing."

As I quiet my being through spiritual breathing, I then tune in to my heart. What feelings am I experiencing in the various parts of me?

I'm feeling anxious about my meeting this morning.
I'm feeling worried about a financial decision.
I'm trying to figure out this problem at work.
I'm feeling disconnected from my wife.
I'm feeling excited about our trip next week.

In these moments, I am simply answering the question, *Where am I?* This is not about passing judgment on ourselves for what we are feeling, or labeling things as good or bad, helpful or unhelpful. This is not about fixing or lecturing ourselves.

This is about awareness. This is about *connecting* to our hearts rather than ignoring our hearts.

If the idea of tuning in to emotions is new to you, that's okay. You can grow in this. I sometimes use an acrostic to help me identify one of six basic human emotions I might be feeling. S-H-A-D-E-S. Am I **S**ad? **H**appy? **A**ngry? **D**isgusted? **E**xcited? **S**cared? Having general categories for emotions can help us learn how to identify what we are feeling.

Now, I realize that for many of you, being present to your heart like this may feel awkward and uncomfortable. That's okay. You are learning how to connect with your heart. Don't give up. Keep practicing this connection to your heart, because it provides a foundation for your experience of intimacy with Jesus.

Remember what we said earlier—God wants to meet us where we *really* are, not where we think we are supposed to be. Stillness enables us to slow down long enough to allow God to ask us this all-important question: *"Where are you, really? What are you feeling, thinking, experiencing?"* It's in this *real* place that a door is opened for a deeper connection with the intimate God.

Being Present to Jesus

The third aspect of practicing stillness is *being present to Jesus*. When we slow down long enough to tune in to where *we* are, we are then able to welcome Jesus into that place. The practice of stillness transitions our relationship with God from the superficial to the authentic.

We meet Jesus where we really are, which can feel a bit scary to many of us. How will Jesus respond to these parts of me that are fearful, confused, discouraged, ashamed?

We know how He will respond.

Our God is a God of compassion. After Adam and Eve's mess-up, God didn't say to them, *"Why did you screw up so badly? How could you be so stupid?"* No. He simply asked them, *"Where are you?"* He wanted to meet them in their failure and shame. Jesus compassionately moves toward all the parts of us. He wants to meet us right where we are.

Stillness creates space for an authentic encounter with God.

Doesn't that sound amazing? Being with Jesus just as you are. No hiding. No secrets. No trying to look spiritual. Nope. Just being *you* in the presence of Him. That's true intimacy.

In this intimate place of stillness, we can release to God any anxious or troubled parts of us. In my times of stillness, I find myself frequently using a prayer that John Eldredge encourages us to pray in times of stillness: "I give everyone and everything to You, God. I give everyone and everything to You."[8]

Take a moment and practice saying that prayer right now.

Can you feel a peace come upon you in that simple prayer of release? Stillness provides this sacred space to offer our authentic selves to God.

Also, in stillness we give room for our hearts to more deeply experience what we learned about in last week's content—the reality of God's face being turned toward us and His love being poured out within us. In stillness we can rest in His love. We can better hear His Spirit whisper to our heart, *"You are mine. I love you."*

My soul needs that . . . regularly. Your soul does as well. In the midst of the relentless hurry and busyness and stress and distractions of our world, our souls need to regularly experience how much Jesus loves us. Stillness provides for us that opportunity.

The natural result of this experience of Jesus' love in our times of stillness will often be a stirring in our heart to express our love for Him. *Jesus, I love You. I really love You.*

The practice of stillness creates space in our lives for an authentic, loving connection with Jesus. That sounds a whole lot like intimacy, doesn't it? Stillness is the foundation for intimacy with Jesus.

How Do We Practice Stillness?

The short answer? Just do it. There are no shortcuts or secrets on this one. We learn by doing. Now, don't freak out thinking that this must take a huge amount of time. It doesn't. Honestly, a few minutes daily of stillness can be significantly transformative in your life.

In your exercises this week, you will have three specific opportunities to practice stillness. For some of you, the practice of stillness will feel easy. For others, it will be challenging. You may initially feel anxious or distracted. That's totally normal.

Give yourself grace. Rather than feeling ashamed or trying to fight against those things, welcome Jesus into them. Every distracted thought becomes an opportunity to return once again to a Savior who loves you and longs to be with you.

So don't be discouraged. Keep practicing stillness. You will get better at it, and your soul will be grateful.

Because this practice is foundational to our experience of intimacy with Jesus, it will be incorporated into each of the exercises in the remaining weeks. By the end of this journey, the practice of stillness will hopefully be an integral part of the rhythm of your life.

Have a great week!

Exercises

EXERCISE ONE

Carve out a few minutes where you can be alone in a quiet place with no distractions (including turning off your cell phone).

Take a few deep breaths. Attach the following prayer to each inhale and exhale. "Holy Spirit" (inhale), "breathe on me" (exhale). Repeat this a few times.

Now take a couple of minutes to be present to yourself. Where are you right now? Be attentive to the scattered parts of you. What parts of you are "around the table"? What thoughts or emotions (remember S-H-A-D-E-S) are you currently experiencing or have you experienced in the last day or two?

Don't beat yourself up for things you are feeling. Don't run from these emotions. Be present to your heart.

Now that you are fully present to yourself in this moment, welcome Jesus into that authentic, real space. Imagine yourself in a peaceful place and Jesus coming to sit in front of you. Say to Him, *"Jesus, I give everything and everyone to You."*

Open your heart afresh to experience His delight in you. (Feel free to imagine yourself again in the prodigal son story or imagine Jesus expressing His tender love for you.)

Take some time to enjoy His love.

Tell Him that you love Him.

EXERCISE TWO

Carve out a few minutes today where you can be alone in a quiet place with no distractions. Don't hurry this.

Take a minute for spiritual breathing. "Abba Father" (inhale), "I belong to You" (exhale). Repeat this a few times.

Now ask yourself, *Where am I?* Pay attention to the thoughts and emotions that parts of you are feeling.

Now imagine that Jesus' face is turned toward you and that He delights in you.

Imagine that He says to you, *"I see you. I understand what you are going through."* How does it feel to have Him say that to you?

Say to Him, *"I give everything and everyone to You."* Feel free to repeat this prayer to Him as often as you'd like.

Take a few moments and express to Him your love for Him.

EXERCISE THREE

Carve out a few minutes today where you can be alone in a quiet place with no distractions.

Do at least one minute of spiritual breathing.

Now ask yourself, *Where am I?* Be attentive to the parts of you that surface. What emotions and thoughts are you carrying?

Now say to Him, *"Jesus, I give everything and everyone to You."* Repeat that prayer as often as necessary.

As you release all these things to Him, open your heart to receive His love for you. Imagine Him holding you or His presence surrounding you. Feel His love for you. Enjoy His delight in you.

Now express your love for Him.

Recommended Resources for Further Exploration

Wholeheartedness: Busyness, Exhaustion, and Healing the Divided Self by Chuck DeGroat

The Ruthless Elimination of Hurry: How to Stay Emotionally Healthy and Spiritually Alive in the Chaos of the Modern World by John Mark Comer

WEEK THREE

Listening to Jesus

Pause to Review

Before starting the content of this chapter, take a moment to pause and reflect on the following questions:

- Were you able to create space in your life to slow down and practice being present in the moment?

- How was your experience of stillness? Was it difficult? Challenging? Meaningful?

Don't be discouraged if your initial attempts at stillness were a struggle. Learning to be present to our hearts is a new experience for many of us. It will get easier with practice . . . and it will open a door for deepening your connection with Jesus.

This Week

Something incredibly powerful can happen when our souls are quieted in stillness. As we tune in to our real selves, we are better able to listen to the voice of God speaking to our hearts.

This was the prophet Elijah's experience. After heading into the wilderness for some much-needed stillness in the midst of his discouragement and fear, God tells him to stand outside the cave he was in:

> Then a great and powerful wind tore the mountains apart and shattered the rocks before the LORD, but the LORD was not in the wind. After the wind there was an earthquake, but the LORD was not in the earthquake. After the earthquake came a fire, but the LORD was not in the fire. And after the fire came a gentle whisper. (1 Kings 19:11–12)

The Lord was in the whisper.

Elijah's experience of stillness opened the door for him to better hear the Lord's voice. I wonder if part of our struggle to hear God's voice is because our souls are rarely quiet enough to hear His whisper.

If God spoke to us by shouting, we wouldn't need stillness. If someone is shouting at you, their voice is nearly impossible to ignore. But what if they are whispering? You have to lean in to hear them.

Maybe that's why God's primary mode of communication with us is through a whisper. He wants us to slow down and lean in. He wants us to quiet our souls. He wants us to "be still, and know that I am God" (Psalm 46:10). The knowing comes *after* the stillness.

We see a powerful example of this in the life of Jesus in Mark 1. Early in the morning, Jesus gets up and finds a solitary place to pray. (We will look at the practice of prayer next week.)

In this place of stillness, His disciples eventually come find Him and say, "Everyone is looking for you" (Mark 1:37). In other words, "We have an agenda for you. There are lots of people here who need you."

Look carefully at Jesus' response: "Let us go somewhere else—to the nearby villages—so I can preach there also. That is why I have come" (Mark 1:38). In His time of stillness, Jesus heard His Father's whisper, giving Him clarity regarding His schedule and priorities for that day.

Even Jesus needed stillness in order to clearly hear His Father's whisper.

Listening to the Voice of Jesus

So how can we better hear the whisper of Jesus? The good news is, this is something we can grow in. With practice, each of us can develop our listening skills. When Raylene and I were first married, I was not a good listener. But over time, with intentional practice, my listening skills are improving, deepening our relational connection.

My journey with Jesus has been a similar experience. For the first several years of my Christian life, listening to God's whisper wasn't even on my radar. In my time with Him, I was so focused on Bible reading, praying through my list, etc., that I didn't take time to listen. But over time, I have learned to better hear His voice through practice.

There is one foundational skill for being a good listener: Attentiveness. Jesus says in John 10:27, "My sheep *listen* to my voice" (emphasis mine). Did you realize that there is a huge difference between hearing and listening? I remember a conversation with Raylene when, even though I was looking at her and nodding my head, she stopped at one point and asked, "Where are you? You're not listening." She was right. I was hearing the sound of her words, but my mind was somewhere else.

Listening in any relationship requires more than just hearing the sound waves that land in our ear canals. Listening requires attentiveness—choosing to focus our complete attention on the other person.

This is especially true in our relationship with God. A lot of Christians think that God isn't speaking to them, when the reality is, He *is* speaking to them. But He's speaking to them in a way that requires attentiveness. In order to hear God's whisper, you must be still. Stillness enables us to quiet our hearts and minds so that we can be more attentive to His whisper.

Tuning In to the Whisper

What does it mean, practically speaking, to hear the Spirit's whisper? We are talking about something that happens internally, in our spirit. The way the Holy Spirit most often speaks is by dropping into our heart or our mind a thought, an idea, a prompting, a scripture, a picture, a song, or a phrase.

As we are being attentive to our inner being, we now notice these things. It may initially feel like a fleeting thought, something we could easily ignore, and probably have hundreds of times before. But now, because we are being attentive, we choose not to ignore it. We pay attention to it. We see if it gains traction.

Sometimes a fleeting thought is just that—a fleeting thought that goes away as quickly as it came. But other times, what initially feels like a fleeting thought doesn't go away. The more we sit with it, the "weightier" it becomes. Over time, we learn how to better recognize when this prompting is the Lord.

Not long ago, I was praying for one of my adult children, bringing to the Lord a specific request that for years I had been asking Him for. As I began to pray for this again, I sensed a gentle whisper in my spirit. *"I want you to stop praying for that. I've heard your prayer. I've got this."* I knew that thought wasn't from me, because I wanted to keep praying for this need! But I decided to pay attention to the whisper. Over the next few weeks, I prayed for my child but not that specific request. Wouldn't you know that very soon after that, God answered that specific request.

Asking Questions

My ability to hear the Lord's voice increased dramatically when I began incorporating a simple practice into my times of stillness: asking questions. What better way to grow closer in any relationship than to ask a person questions. Questions are a simple yet powerful way to gain access to someone's heart.

Why do you think Jesus asked so many questions in His interactions with His followers?[9] Lectures tend to be one-directional. Questions open the door for genuine dialogue and deeper interaction. Could it be that questions are a key to intimacy? The practice of stillness creates space for us to ask the Lord questions and then to tune in to His whisper.

So, what questions should we ask Him? Ask Him anything! Ask Him whatever is on your heart. As we saw in last week's content, the practice of stillness helps us tune in to what is really going on in our mind and our heart. What are we feeling? What are we worried about?

Why not ask Jesus about those parts of us? And then listen. Pay attention to the thoughts, words, impressions, pictures, scriptures, etc. that immediately come to your heart and mind after you ask. I like to write them down in a journal as I hear them. I can go back and evaluate them later as to whether they align with the Bible (more on that in a moment).

In this initial listening posture, I'm simply trying to pay attention to what I sense is being whispered to my soul. This is a big deal. How often do we stop to pay attention to what God might be whispering to our inner being?

In doing this, I've discovered something simple and yet incredibly significant: God most often speaks to us through our own thoughts. In other words, He doesn't speak to me in Shakespearean language. He speaks to me the way Alan Kraft would say it or hear it.

I love that. It's personal and real. His Spirit and my spirit, His mind and my mind, in the same place, because I have chosen to quiet my heart and listen.

Hearing His Guidance

One of the things we can ask Jesus is a question about direction. Remember earlier in Mark 1, we saw that it was in Jesus' practice of solitude and stillness that God gave Him direction for His next ministry endeavor.

A few months ago, I was needing to make a decision regarding a denominational leadership team I had served on for several years. I was losing my motivation to engage and wasn't even sure

I should continue. I knew I needed to decide, but I just kept kicking the can down the road, uncertain of which way to go.

One day, I mentioned this to my wife, who immediately asked me, "Have you asked Jesus what He wants you to do?" I couldn't believe she would even ask that. I'm a pastor. Of course I had asked Jesus . . . and then I realized, I hadn't. So, the next morning in my practice of stillness, I took out my journal and wrote this question on an empty page: "Jesus, what do You want me to do about this leadership team I am on?" And then I listened.

Within a few moments, I sensed Him whispering to my heart, *"You have abdicated your leadership on this team. I want you to step up and lead."* So, I said yes to what I sensed Him saying to me and then let the other team members know. Two of them responded by saying, "We've known this for months. We were just waiting to see when you would finally ask the Lord about it."

What a powerful lesson for me. I'd spent so much time carrying the weight of this decision but had never once asked Jesus what He wanted me to do. Since saying yes to Him, I have enjoyed seeing the positive impact of that choice.

Quick caveat: as humans, we often have a harder time hearing an answer to a directional question when we are secretly hoping for a particular answer or when the decision is a significant one (new job, getting married, etc.). In those situations, it is wise to confirm His voice through the counsel of others.

Love Questions

I remember the first time I told my wife, Raylene, that I loved her. We had been dating for a few months, and I knew she was the one I wanted to marry. So, as we walked one evening on the twelfth fairway of a nearby golf course (romantic, huh?), I said those three words . . . and then, with my heart laid open, waited for her response. I wanted to know that she felt the same way. (She did, by the way.)

In a love relationship, we want and need to hear this other person tell us how they feel about us. This is also true in our relationship with God. As we saw earlier in week one, a crucial part of the Spirit's job description is to "testify with our spirit that we are God's children" (Romans 8:16). To testify means to speak. The Spirit wants to whisper to our inner being how fully loved we are by God.

Asking the Lord love-related questions provides a great way to hear that afresh. What if, the next time you practice stillness, you ask the Lord, *Jesus, what do You like about me?* and then you listen to His response? Write down whatever thoughts come to mind. You are giving the Spirit room to whisper to your soul the truth of how much He delights in you.

Sometimes we need to hear this whisper in a place of wounding or pain. Not long ago, as I was practicing stillness, I became aware of some deep feelings of insecurity in my own heart. In thinking about that, I had a memory come to mind where someone in my life didn't really listen to me. I realized in this prayer time how hurtful that had been to my heart. In that place of wounding, my heart subconsciously concluded that I wasn't worth loving. I began to believe a lie that I had to succeed in order to be valued by others.

So, as tears came to my eyes from this wound, I renounced the lie I had believed, and then I asked Jesus, *What's the truth you want me to know?* This is a portion of what I heard from Him and wrote in my journal: *"I see you. I am listening to you. Your heart matters to Me. I love you for who you are and not just what you can do. I love you for being My son. I am so proud of you."*

It was just what my heart needed to hear. I'm so glad I took some time to ask Jesus to speak to my heart in that very vulnerable place. In stillness we have a beautiful opportunity to listen to Jesus speak His love into the deepest parts of ourselves.

As we continue our journey of intimacy with Jesus in the coming weeks, we will see how our ability to hear the voice of Jesus can have a significant impact upon our experience of prayer and our engagement in Scripture. But for now, I simply want you to practice listening to Jesus in your times of stillness, allowing your intimacy with Him to deepen.

How Do We Know If What We Hear Is Actually from God?

Before concluding this week's content, I want to address a common concern. How do we know if what we are hearing is from God? Obviously, none of us want to be deceived or misled. Might this be opening a door that could lead to spiritual danger?

The reality is, there are all sorts of good things that can be misused and lead to spiritual danger. People have used the Bible to justify things like slavery. Some churches have become abusive, harmful communities due to unhealthy leadership. Does that mean we throw out the Bible or the concept of church leadership simply because these things can and have been misused? Of course not.

Rather, we fully engage in these things but use discernment in doing so. Discernment provides necessary guardrails for our spiritual journey. Does God still speak? Absolutely. Do we need to use discernment in hearing His voice? Absolutely.

And remember, we are talking about a love relationship. Isn't it interesting how Jesus uses the language of sheep and a shepherd to describe our relationship with Him? I don't know much about sheep, but I hear they are not very smart and are prone to wander. What does a good shepherd do when a sheep begins to wander? The shepherd lovingly and gently gets them back on track.

Jesus wants to help us listen to Him. If we happen to hear incorrectly, He is eager to guide us back to the path He has for us. So, let's continue to learn how to recognize our Good Shepherd's voice.

When we think we hear something from the Lord, we can use our discernment to determine whether this is from God. In my previous book, I describe four discernment tests we can use.[10]

1. **The Scripture Test**: Does this violate any principle in the Bible?
2. **The Tone Test:** Does this feel forceful or condemning? Is this consistent with what we know of God's character?
3. **The Resonance Test:** Does this resonate with my heart? Does it bring peace and conviction? Or does it cause confusion or fear? Does it resonate with those who know me well?
4. **The Fruit Test:** Does this bear positive fruit in my life or the life of the person I share this word with?

Whenever we sense the Lord whispering something to our heart, these four questions can provide some discernment guardrails to help guide us. This kind of testing is something the Lord expects us to do. In 1 Thessalonians 5:19–21 (NLT) Paul urges us, "Do not stifle the Holy Spirit. Do not scoff at prophecies, but test everything that is said. Hold on to what is good."

Let me reiterate what I said earlier: God eagerly wants to help us learn how to listen better to Him.[11] The practice of stillness provides a beautiful opportunity to do just that. In your exercises this week, we will be learning how to listen better to our intimate God.

Exercises

Have a journal or notebook with you during these exercises to write down whatever you are hearing.

EXERCISE ONE

Begin your practice of stillness with some spiritual breathing, attaching a simple prayer to your inhale and exhale.

Now be present to your inner being. What parts of you are needing to be seen? What emotions or thoughts are you experiencing? Acknowledge them with compassion.

Now be present to the Lord. Be aware of His presence with you. Feel free to imagine Jesus standing before you or sitting beside you. Enjoy His presence. Express your love for Him.

After enjoying His presence for a few moments, practice listening by asking Him this question:

Jesus, when You look at me, what do You see?

Write down whatever you hear Him say.

Thank Him for His presence with you.

EXERCISE TWO

Begin your practice of stillness with some spiritual breathing.

Now be present to your inner being. What parts of you are needing to be seen? What emotions or thoughts are you experiencing? Acknowledge them with compassion.

Be aware of Jesus' presence with you. Enjoy Him.

Think of one of the emotions you are experiencing. What would it look like to process that emotion in the Lord's presence? Ask Him if there is anything He wants to say to you about that emotion.

If it is a negative emotion, ask the Lord, *Is there a lie or false perspective that I am believing in this situation?* Then take a minute or two just to listen.

If you hear anything, write it down. If it becomes clear that you're being told or are telling yourself a lie, renounce it. *Jesus, I renounce this lie that I have been believing that I will never measure up . . .* or *that You don't have good things for me.*

For each lie you renounced, now ask Him, *Jesus, what is the truth You want me to know?*

Write down what you hear.

EXERCISE THREE

Practice stillness (spiritual breathing, being present to yourself).

Now be aware of Jesus' presence with you. Enjoy His presence.

Think of a person you would like to pray for. Imagine them standing in a room. Now imagine that Jesus enters into that room and comes up to them. Ask Him, *Lord Jesus, what do You want to do for this person?*

Pay attention to what Jesus does in this picture.

Take a moment and pray for them what Jesus did for them in this picture in your mind.

If you feel a freedom to do so, share with this person what you heard the Lord saying to you.

Recommended Resources for Further Exploration

Can You Hear Me?: Tuning in to the God Who Speaks by Brad Jersak
More: When a Little Bit of the Spirit Is Not Enough by Alan Kraft

WEEK FOUR

Prayer

Pause to Review

For the last three weeks, you have been laying a crucial foundation for a life of intimacy with Jesus. The practice of stillness enables us to experience the Lord's love in a powerful way, as we tune in to our own hearts and then welcome the presence of Jesus into that place.

- Thinking about this past week, how fully did you experience the Lord's love for you?

- How was your experience of listening to Jesus in your times of stillness?

This Week

The foundational practice of stillness opens a door for us to experience a second core practice that can deepen our connection with Jesus: the practice of prayer. For Jesus, the practices of stillness and prayer go hand in hand. We read in Luke 5,

"Yet the news about him spread all the more, so that crowds of people came to hear him and to be healed of their sicknesses. But Jesus often withdrew to lonely places and prayed." (Luke 5:15–16)

Luke describes Jesus withdrawing to solitary places—places where He could be alone with God and experience stillness. But in that place, He also experienced something else. Jesus prayed.

Think about that. Jesus, the perfect Son of God, God in the flesh, carved out time in His life for prayer. And not just occasionally. Luke tells us that Jesus often withdrew to lonely places to pray. This was a regular part of His life rhythm, His routine.

In the midst of a very demanding schedule with people constantly needing things from Him, Jesus knew He needed time with His heavenly Father. For Jesus, prayer was not a ritual or duty. It was rooted in relationship. Jesus prayed as a way of connecting with and partnering with His heavenly Father.

And what's amazing is that Jesus invites us into this same experience. Not only that, He shows us how. Jesus shares with us exactly how He prayed on those cold, dark mornings in the wilderness.

How Jesus Prayed

"This, then, is how you should pray: Our Father in heaven, hallowed be your name, your kingdom come, your will be done, on earth as it is in heaven. Give us today our daily bread. And forgive us our debts, as we also have forgiven our debtors. And lead us not into temptation, but deliver us from the evil one." (Matthew 6:9–13)

In this passage, Jesus teaches us how to pray. This is like getting a cooking lesson from Gordon Ramsay or a singing lesson from Carrie Underwood. In this passage, Jesus our Savior gives us this very personal and specific window into what a healthy prayer life looks like. Unfortunately, many Christians miss the significance of this prayer by reducing it to something to be recited.

But it is so much more than that.

For centuries in the church, this prayer has been recognized as a template to help us learn how to pray. This prayer has had a profound impact on my experience of prayer. It all started in a conversation years ago with a pastor friend of mine whose prayer life I deeply admired. As we were riding in a car together, I asked him, "Brian, what has been the most helpful resource for you in developing your life of prayer?"

I expected him to give me the name of a book or some video teaching to watch. Without hesitation, he responded, "It's when I learned to pray the Lord's Prayer, using the prayer of Jesus as my own pattern for praying."

I was so intrigued by his answer that I immediately began doing this in my own prayer time. I've never stopped. This continues to be my primary paradigm for my practice of prayer. What I love about using it in this way is that it shows us what Jesus considered to be the crucial elements of a healthy prayer life.

Sometimes we can get into a rut in our praying. We only pray for ourselves or maybe for others, but we miss some other important aspects of prayer. Imagine doing an exercise program that only focuses on your biceps because you like working that particular muscle. The result? You will have amazing biceps . . .

but what about your abs? Or your lower body? In a good exercise program for optimal health, you focus on multiple areas.

The Lord's Prayer provides a pathway on which we can run and thrive in prayer. Whether you are new to prayer or have been praying for years, using this prayer can add vibrancy to your prayer life and a deeper experience of intimacy with Jesus.

The Lord's Prayer Unpacked

In the Lord's Prayer, there are six areas on which Jesus focuses. Here is a diagram I use to help people see all the parts of this prayer.

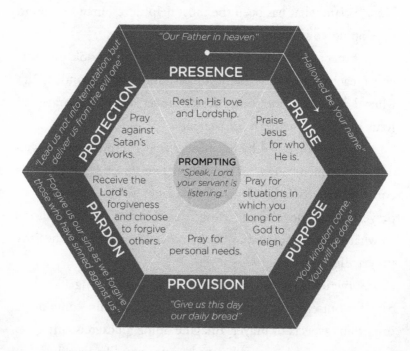

Presence

The first area of focus is presence. Jesus begins with the words "Our Father in heaven" (Matthew 6:9). What is He doing here? He is focusing our hearts on the presence of God—the One we are praying to. Jesus wants us to know what this God is like, so He begins by calling Him "Father." No Jew would ever refer to God in this personal of a way, but Jesus did.

Jesus wants you to know, right off the bat, that you are praying to a Father who loves you and delights in you (remember week one?). By beginning your prayers in this way, you will be continually establishing in your heart and mind an accurate perception of how God feels about you.

Jesus also reveals that our Father God is in heaven. In other words, He sits enthroned as Lord of the universe. We are not praying to a God who is too busy, distracted, uncaring, or emotionally distant. We are not praying to a God who is unable to help us in our need.

We are praying to a God who loves us beyond measure and who can do beyond what we could ask or imagine. Just knowing that makes me want to pray even more!

Praise

Jesus then prays, "Hallowed be your name" (Matthew 6:9). From a biblical perspective, someone's name represents their character. The word *hallowed* means holy, representing the fullness and perfection of all of God's attributes.

To focus on God's name as holy is an invitation for us to express praise to God for who He is and what He has done. Praise is not praise unless it is expressed. We can feel and think all sorts of wonderful things toward someone, but until we express that to them, we have not entered into praise.

In this section of this prayer, we express praise to God for specific attributes of His character—His love, compassion, faithfulness, power, etc. This is also a wonderful opportunity to express gratitude to God for specific things He has done in your life, which helps cultivate joy in our hearts.

Purpose

The third area of prayer that Jesus invites us to experience focuses on God's kingdom purpose. Jesus prays, "Your kingdom come, your will be done on earth as it is in heaven" (Matthew 6:10).

Jesus frequently talked about the kingdom of God—but not simply as a future reality in heaven. The word *kingdom* refers to whatever is under the rule of a king. The kingdom of God is wherever Jesus' authority, influence, and power are being experienced right now.

So, when Jesus urges us to pray, "Your kingdom come, your will be done," He is inviting us to partner with Him in seeing God's influence and power manifest in our world right now. How cool is that?

In this part of our prayer time, we're thinking of people or situations where God's power is needed—to heal a marriage or provide a job or break an addiction in someone's life. We're praying for our neighbors to come to Christ. We're praying for the horrors of sex trafficking to be eradicated. We are partnering with God to bring His kingdom to this earth right now—to bring healing, life, peace, and freedom.

When I'm in this part of the Lord's Prayer, I often pray for friends who have specific needs—for healing in their marriage, for cancer to be gone, for them to come to know Christ. I also pray for my wife and family as well as our church.

This "your kingdom come" prayer can also be a place where we wrestle with God about something. Remember how Jesus, in the garden of Gethsemane, prayed, "Yet not as I will, but as you will" (Matthew 26:39). Sometimes we are involved in the answer to this prayer. Praying "your kingdom come" means asking God, *Is there any role I play in bringing the kingdom into this situation? Is there anything You are calling me to do to help bring Your presence?* And then we listen to and obey the Holy Spirit.

This is such a powerful part of our prayer time, because we get to partner with God in boldly asking for His kingdom to come to the people and circumstances around us.

Provision

The fourth theme in this prayer focuses on provision. Jesus prays, "Give us today our daily bread" (Matthew 6:11). Notice the beautiful shift that happens here. The first three areas of the Lord's Prayer are focused on God—who He is and where His kingdom is needed.

But beginning in the second half of this Lord's Prayer, Jesus encourages us to get personal. Where do we need His work in *our* lives? Jesus encourages us to pray about our daily needs. What a beautiful reminder that God cares about our practical, personal, everyday needs . . . like bread, for instance. God cares about the "little" things that we care about.

Often in our lives, we don't pray about certain needs because they feel too trivial to bring to God's attention. But nothing is too trivial to bring to our Father's attention.

If we care about it, He cares about it.

And it's not only about needs. God cares about what you want. Maybe there are heart desires you have that you have never prayed about. Why not? God cares about your heart.

Pardon

The fifth part of Jesus' prayer focuses on pardon, the need for forgiveness. "And forgive us our debts, as we also have forgiven our debtors" (Matthew 6:12).

I love the fact that Jesus includes this. How often do we fall into the trap of thinking that, because we recently messed up in some area of our lives, we can't pray. We're not good enough or holy enough. We're tainted by sin, so we can't approach God . . . at least for a few days. But here, Jesus reminds us of something very important about prayer.

Prayer is for sinners.

We don't have to clean up our lives in order to pray. No, we are praying to a God who forgives us. So Jesus urges us to take some time in prayer to confess any sinful actions in our lives—not so that we beat ourselves up but so that we *experience* His forgiveness.

In this part of our prayer time, we ask the Lord if there are any sins we need to confess to Him, and then we wait to see if the Holy Spirit brings anything to mind. If so, we confess that sin and ask Jesus to forgive us and cleanse us of all unrighteousness. We receive His grace.

Once we experience afresh Jesus' forgiveness for our sins, guess what our hearts are now better able to do? To forgive those who have sinned against us, which is what Jesus mentions next: "as we forgive our debtors" (Matthew 6:12).

Whenever we pray, Jesus urges us to include a time in which we examine our heart to see if we are harboring bitterness toward anyone and we choose to forgive them. We ask, *Jesus, is there anyone I need to forgive?*

If He brings someone to mind, we choose to forgive them. We bring that offense to the cross and leave it with Jesus. (For more details about how to forgive someone, see exercise two at the end of this week's content.)

Notice how the relational aspect of prayer includes our relationships with others. Honestly, I would prefer to skip this part and hold on to my bitterness toward someone who hurt me.

But God doesn't want us harboring bitterness toward others because of the toxic impact on us spiritually. By putting forgiveness in the Lord's Prayer, Jesus highlights the importance of our relationships being healthy.

Protection

The sixth area in this prayer is protection. Jesus prays, "And lead us not into temptation, but deliver us from the evil one" (Matthew 6:13). Jesus wants us to remember that we are in a battle with a very real spiritual enemy who is evil and who wants to do all he can to damage the work of God in us. By doing so, he robs God of glory.

One of the most powerful weapons we have against this enemy is prayer. We can't fight this enemy on our own. We need the power of God working on our behalf, which is why Jesus includes this final section focusing on our spiritual warfare.

Notice the two things Jesus prays for here. First, we pray in the name of Jesus for strength to resist temptation: "Lead us not into temptation" (Matthew 6:13). These words seem so familiar to us, but how often do we actually pray for God's help in resisting specific areas of sin in our lives?

Second, we pray for deliverance from the evil one. For me, this includes praying for Jesus' protection over my life, family, church, etc. If you are uncertain how to pray spiritual warfare prayers, I have found great help in John Eldredge's Daily Prayer.[12]

————

Those are the six areas Jesus mentions in the Lord's Prayer: Presence, Praise, Purpose, Provision, Pardon, Protection. If you look back at the diagram on page 56, you will notice an important word strategically placed in the center of it: Prompting.

During our entire prayer time, we want to be attentive to the Holy Spirit's voice, as we explored last week. What may the Holy Spirit want to say to us in any of these areas? For instance, who to pray for in terms of His kingdom coming, or who we need to forgive, or how we can bring the kingdom to someone else, etc.

This is the relational aspect of prayer that drew Jesus into prayer. Prayer is not a monologue; it is a dialogue. It's a conversation. We're not simply checking prayer items off a list. We are continually opening our heart to God's heart.

Just the other day I was praying for someone and stopped to ask, *God, how do You want me to pray for this person?* God brought to my mind a picture that helped shape my praying for this person. Rather than assuming we know what to pray for when we pray for someone, we can ask Jesus what is on His heart for them.

This week in the exercises, you will be learning to pray the way Jesus taught us to pray, using His prayer as a guide or template for prayer.

Now, please hear me. This is not the only way to pray. Nor is it intended to be a legalistic ritual you must go through anytime you pray. I know for some of you, thinking about praying through a pattern like this already feels restrictive and maybe even unmotivating. I get that.

But before you dismiss this section, I'd like for you to think about this prayer as a new cooking recipe you are trying. The first few times you cook this dish, you follow the recipe closely. But soon you begin thinking about flavors and ingredients you want to add to make it your own. You begin experimenting with the recipe so that it eventually reflects your tastes and desires.

Think of the Lord's Prayer as a recipe for an amazing dish. The ingredients are all strategically placed there for a purpose. I want you to take some time to get comfortable with the ingredients as you do the exercises and pray through this prayer.

But once you are comfortable with the ingredients, feel free to adapt this prayer for your own prayer life. Maybe you pray through this prayer over the course of a week. Maybe you change up the order or pray only a few ingredients at certain times. The important thing, according to Jesus, is that these six areas are a regular part of your prayer life with Him.

In the first two exercises for this week's content, you will be praying through portions of this prayer, with the goal being that by exercise three, you will be praying through the entire prayer in one sitting. We will then use this prayer in our exercises throughout the rest of this journey.

You will also notice that in each exercise, we combine this experience of the Lord's Prayer with the practices of stillness. The two fit seamlessly together.

Have a great week as you grow in your practice of prayer!

Exercises

EXERCISE ONE

Stillness

Begin with a time of stillness. As you quiet your heart through spiritual breathing, ask yourself, *Where am I? Where is my heart today?*

Now welcome Jesus into that space. Feel free to use your imagination to envision Him being with you.

Prayer

Pray through the first three areas of the Lord's Prayer.

Presence: *Our Father in heaven*

As we transition from stillness to the Lord's Prayer, intentionally envision God as your loving Father. He delights in you. He is so grateful to be with you right now. Enjoy being in His love. Feel free to imagine His love surrounding you.

Take a few moments to also envision God being in heaven on His throne. Nothing is too difficult for Him.

Imagine in your mind that as you approach His throne in prayer, He stops whatever He is doing, and He looks at you and says, *"My child, I am here for you. I am listening to you. It is so good to be together."*

Enjoy His loving and powerful presence with you.

Praise: *Hallowed be Your name.*

Take some time to reflect on who Jesus is. What names or attributes come to mind? (compassionate, loving, holy, Savior, etc.). Express praise to Him for each of these attributes or names that comes to mind.

Take some time to reflect on a specific blessing God has provided for you. As you think about that blessing, allow your mind to savor it, to enjoy it.

Now thank God specifically for those blessings.

Purpose: *Your kingdom come, Your will be done, on earth as it is in heaven.*

What needs/situations/areas break your heart? Where do you long to see God's kingdom come? Make a list of those things.

Take a moment and ask God to move powerfully in each of those areas. Ask for His kingdom, His rule, to come into each situation.

After doing that, ask God, *Is there anything You want me to do to bring Your kingdom into any of these situations?* Stop and listen.

Close your time in prayer.

EXERCISE TWO

Stillness
Begin with the practice of stillness as described in Exercise One.

Prayer
Pray through the next three areas of the Lord's Prayer.

Provision: *Give me this day my daily bread.*

Think of a personal need that you have, maybe something you have never prayed about because it has felt too trivial to bring to God. Take a few moments and bring that to God in prayer. Tell Him what you long for and need. Rest in the truth that He hears you and sees you.

Pardon: *Forgive my sins as I forgive those who have sinned against me.*

Ask the Holy Spirit, *Is there any sin I need to confess to You?* For each sin He brings to mind, confess and repent of it. Ask for His forgiveness and cleansing.

Think for a moment about how God has completely forgiven that sin. It is forgotten by Him, completely washed away. It no longer defines you. You no longer have to carry the guilt of that sin.

Ask the Holy Spirit, *Is there anyone I need to forgive? Is there anyone I am harboring bitterness toward?*

If someone comes to mind, prayerfully walk through the steps of forgiveness:

> **A—Acknowledge the hurt**. Forgiveness is not minimizing or ignoring what happened. It is acknowledging to God the hurt. For example, *God, when my father called me a loser, it hurt me deeply. I felt rejected, alone, etc.* Be specific.

> **B—Bring it to the cross**. In this step, we bring this offense to the cross, where Jesus died for sin, and we leave it there. For example, *Jesus, I bring this offense to the cross. I don't want to carry it any longer. I choose to let go of my right to retaliate. I forgive this person.*

C—Confess any sinful responses you have had. Even though we were the ones who were hurt, we often respond to this hurt in sinful ways. We need to confess that to Jesus. For example, *Jesus, I ask for forgiveness for the hatred and bitterness I have held against this person,* or, *I confess the lie I embraced that I would never amount to anything.*

Receive Jesus' forgiveness for these sins, renounce any lies you have believed, and break any past vows you have made in response to this hurt.

Now pray God's blessing upon the person you have forgiven.

Thank God for His forgiveness.

Protection: *Lead me not into temptation, but deliver me from the evil one.*

Pray for strength to resist temptations that you face—and not just the obvious ones. How about the temptation to shade the truth in conversations in order to look better in the eyes of your boss, or the temptation to binge-watch television shows late into the night, which squeezes out your time for God? Let the Spirit reveal areas of temptation for you.

Pray for the protection of Jesus over your life, your relationships, your church, etc.

EXERCISE THREE

Stillness
Begin with a time of stillness.

Prayer
Pray through each of these areas (see the previous two exercises for more detail on these):

Presence
Praise
Purpose
Provision
Pardon
Protection

You have just prayed through the Lord's Prayer!

EXTRA EXERCISE
Use the diagram to teach someone (your spouse, your children, a friend, your small group) how to pray through the Lord's Prayer. Go through each of the six areas, explain them, and then pray through them with this person.

Recommended Resources for Further Exploration

Moving Mountains: Praying with Passion, Confidence, and Authority by John Eldredge

A Praying Life: Connecting with God in a Distracting World by Paul Miller

WEEK FIVE

Engaging in Scripture

Pause to Review

You are at week five of this journey of deeper connection with Jesus. Way to go! So far in this journey, we have been growing in two beautiful and transformative core spiritual practices: stillness and prayer.

In stillness, we take time to slow down and tune in to our own hearts, in order to be fully present and attentive to God, welcoming Jesus into every part of us. We quiet our souls to listen to His whisper. That practice of stillness opens the door for a relationally engaging experience of prayer with God.

- How are you feeling about your experience of stillness and prayer over the past few weeks?

- What are you hearing God speak to your heart?

This Week

You've got to figure that any discussion of spiritual practices and growing in our relationship with Jesus is going to include some discussion about the Bible.

So now that we have nailed down this week's topic, could we allow for some brutal honesty?

Most Christians know that they *should* spend time in the Bible, but we often don't. Many of us know the importance of the Bible, but we struggle to *connect* with the Bible. And understandably so.

The Bible is a complex library of books, written over several centuries, in cultures far removed from ours. It is a book that has many passages that are hard to understand, including some archaic laws (about things like oxen, blood sacrifices, and clothing) and episodes of violence that are troubling to a modern-day person.

So why are we to give this book such an elevated position in our spiritual journey as Christians? Here's the simple answer: because Jesus did.

Jesus and the Scriptures

Jesus had an incredibly high view of His Bible, which is our Old Testament. Jesus taught from it. He memorized it. He quoted it. He viewed it as the authoritative Word of God. He practiced it. He valued it. He leaned on it in times of difficulty.

Jesus loved the Scriptures and relied upon them.

This is an important truth to grasp. Sometimes we may find ourselves losing our motivation to engage in the Bible because of a disconnect we feel with certain difficult passages. We may even start to have doubts about our faith because we can't understand something.

But ultimately our faith is in the person of Jesus, not in our ability to understand every passage in the Bible. This takes the pressure off. We can still love and engage with the Bible as God's inspired Word without feeling the need to explain or defend every part of it.

When we look at how Jesus viewed the Bible, we discover a game-changing answer to this question of why we are to engage in Scripture. From Jesus' perspective, the Bible has a very specific purpose. He explains this purpose in a conversation with two disciples walking to the city of Emmaus: "And beginning with Moses and all the Prophets, he explained to them what was said in all the Scriptures concerning himself" (Luke 24:27). Everything in the Old Testament ultimately points to Jesus.

He is the point.

Which means that the ultimate reason we engage in Scripture is because when we do so, we get to know Jesus better. It helps us experience a deepening intimacy with Him. In other words, our engagement with Scripture is intended to be a *relational* experience. If our reading of Scripture is not fueling a deeper love for Jesus, we are missing the point.

Check out what Jesus once said to the Pharisees, who knew their Bible backward and forward. "You study the Scriptures diligently because you think that in them you have eternal life. These are the very Scriptures that testify about me, yet you refuse to come to me to have life" (John 5:39–40).

Ouch. That had to hurt. Jesus is saying that, in all their diligent study of Scripture, they missed the point of their Scriptures. Jesus. Jesus is the point of every Scripture.

And here's what's scary: We can make the same mistake the Pharisees made. We can diligently study the Bible, filling our journals with notes and charts and Greek word definitions . . . and completely miss the point.

To put it bluntly—who cares if I know what the seals and bowls in the book of Revelation represent if I'm not demonstrating love toward the people around me? Who cares if I've memorized the entire book of Philippians if my love for Jesus isn't growing?

Contrast Jesus' rebuke of the Pharisees to the response of the two followers on the road to Emmaus: "Were not our hearts burning within us while he talked with us on the road and opened the Scriptures to us?" (Luke 24:32).

That's what I want. I want my heart to burn within me when I read Scripture. I want my love for Jesus to deepen. I want my relationship with Him to grow. I'm guessing you want that as well; otherwise, you wouldn't still be reading.

Engaging the Bible

What is it that opens the door for us to be transformed in this way by the Bible? It's the spiritual practice of Scripture meditation. One of the most vivid pictures of the power of meditating on God's Word is found in Psalm 1.

> Blessed is the one who does not walk in step with the wicked
> or stand in the way that sinners take or sit in the company

of mockers, but whose delight is in the law of the LORD, and who meditates on his law day and night. That person is like a tree planted by streams of water, which yields its fruit in season and whose leaf does not wither—whatever they do prospers. Not so the wicked! They are like chaff that the wind blows away. (Psalm 1:1–4)

In this psalm, we see a vivid contrast between someone whose life is like chaff—being blown here and there, no stability, or fruitfulness—and a person whose life is like a tree planted by a stream of water. Stable. Thriving even in difficulty and drought.

What is it that makes the difference between these two very different experiences of life? The psalmist tells us. Blessed is the person who delights in God's Word and *meditates* on it day and night. This word *meditate* is the Hebrew word *hagah*, which means to ponder, to muse, to imagine, to reflect upon, to let ruminate.

Or for anyone who likes to grill . . . to marinate. Meditating on Scripture is the difference between sprinkling some seasoning on a steak while it's cooking or letting a steak marinate for hours in soy sauce and ginger before placing it on the grill. When a steak is allowed to marinate in these seasonings, the flavor comes alive because it's had time to permeate the meat.

To meditate on Scripture is like that—allowing room for the Word to permeate our being, to settle into our soul so that the grace and truth of Jesus become more real to us, more alive in us. This is not speed-reading. Rather, we're intentionally slowing down in the passage and allowing it to speak deeply to us.

In this experience, the Bible is no longer simply a source of information. It becomes a *relational* and *transformative* experience, in which the Holy Spirit uses the Word to point us to Jesus.

Do you see why this is such a powerful practice? Scripture meditation enables us to not be like chaff that is blown here and there by the prevailing breezes of our culture but to become more deeply rooted in Jesus.

How To Meditate on the Bible

In this week's exercises, you are going to have the opportunity to engage in this powerful practice. So let me share a few practical things I have found helpful in my own experience of Scripture meditation.

1. Carve out a regular time for this in your life rhythm.

Just like we talked about with stillness and prayer, regular Bible meditation won't happen automatically. We must create space in our lives for this. Now the good news is, this practice of Scripture meditation fits well with the practice of stillness and prayer that we have already been experiencing. Once we've experienced stillness and prayer, our hearts are open to engage in a passage of Scripture, letting the Lord speak to us through that passage.

2. Have a Bible reading plan.

I find it helpful to have a Bible reading plan in place, so that when I set aside this time, I don't have to figure out what passage to read that day. That can feel overwhelming. The Bible is a long book—more accurately, it's an extensive library of books. Having to decide where to read that day can be a barrier to actually jumping into a passage of Scripture. That's why I like to have a plan in place so that I know what passage I will be reading.

There are many Bible reading plans available, based on particular books, topics, or time available. The YouVersion Bible app is a great place to explore a variety of plans.

The plan I have used for years is the *One Year Bible*. The *One Year Bible* is divided up into 365 daily readings. Each day's reading has an Old Testament reading, a New Testament reading, a portion of a Psalm, and then a portion of Proverbs.

It's designed to take you through the Bible in a year if you read the entire amount each day, but that is not how I utilize this plan. I'm not trying to get through it in a year. I go at my own pace. I read as far as I want and then stop. The next devotional time I spend with the Lord, I simply pick up where I left off. Sometimes I spend a few days in one specific passage. Again, I'm not in any hurry to get through a book or passage.

What I love about this approach is that I don't have to decide each day where to read. I simply open to where I left off the previous devotional time. I have the *One Year Bible* on my Kindle, which makes this especially easy.

The other benefit to me is that this keeps me on a path that eventually takes me through the whole Bible—however long that takes me. I love the fact that, over a period of every two years or so, I am opening my heart to every word in the Bible, asking God to speak to me from that, rather than only spending time in the sections that are my favorites. The key is to find a plan that works for you and allows you to open your heart to Scripture.

What I am describing here is different from going through a devotional resource that provides a daily passage and explanation for you. There is nothing wrong with those kinds of resources. However, in terms of this practice of Scripture meditation, those devotionals are sort of doing the "work" for you. You are reading what someone else thinks about that passage, which again is not wrong. But in Scripture meditation, our desire is to grow in hearing the Lord speak to *us* directly from His Word—not through another person.

If you are currently using a devotional-type book, I encourage you, during this journey, to practice Scripture meditation as I am describing it so that you know how to engage in Scripture on your own.

Now, for me there are some days when, instead of using the *One Year Bible*, I will go directly to a passage that deals with something I'm currently wrestling with—fear or temptation, etc.—and I will spend my time that day meditating on that passage. But my regular rhythm involves utilizing a plan.

The purpose of having a Bible reading plan is not to restrict you. Rather, it is to provide a pathway for you to engage in Scripture over time. For the rest of this journey, I will be providing a Bible reading "plan" in the exercises each week. But at the end of this journey, we will talk about the importance of you finding a Bible reading plan that works for you.

3. Understand where this passage fits in the larger story.

Whenever we read a passage of Scripture, it helps to know where this passage fits in the larger story of Jesus' redemptive work.

Was this written before Jesus lived on earth or after? To whom is this written?

Also, what kind of literature is this? Is this passage poetry, like the Psalms? Is this passage narrative, telling a story? Is this a letter written from one person to another? You read poetry differently than how you read a newspaper or a textbook. Be aware of the genre of literature you are reading.

In addition, be aware of the culture in which each passage was being written. You may come across some passages that are deeply disturbing, especially in the Old Testament in terms of violence and purity laws. I find it helpful to remind myself that this was not written in twenty-first-century civilization. It was not written *to* us. It was written to a people in a significantly different culture.

We need to be careful that we don't project our twenty-first-century values onto an event that happened three thousand years ago in a Middle Eastern context. Always keep in mind where the passage you are reading fits into the larger story of Jesus and His redemptive work. Remember, Jesus is the point of all of Scripture.

4. Read slowly and prayerfully.

This is the most important aspect of Scripture meditation. This is the "secret sauce" that enables the Bible to transform us. Remember the marinating analogy. Scripture meditation is not speed-reading. It is reading slowly and prayerfully, giving room for the Spirit to speak to us from God's Word.

As I mentioned before, when I'm reading in my *One Year Bible*, I don't feel any obligation to get through each day's reading that day. I simply start reading wherever I left off the day before, and I begin reading slowly, asking the Holy Spirit to speak to me.

As you are reading slowly, pay attention to any words, phrases, or verses that stand out to you. When something "shimmers," settle right there for a while. Don't move on. Stay there. Read it again. Chew on it. Ask God, *What are You saying to me here?* Pay attention to what is being stirred in your soul.

Years ago, I learned an acrostic that highlights the various things God might want to speak to us from a passage: S-P-E-C-K.

Is there a **Sin** I need to confess?
Is there a **Promise** my heart longs to claim?
Is there an **Example** I feel moved to follow?
Is there a **Command** God is asking me to obey?
Is there something I need to **Know** about Jesus?

There are any number of things that the Holy Spirit might want to say to us from the Scripture we are reading. The question is, Are we slowing down in the text and allowing room for the Spirit to speak to us?

One of the ways that Christians have experienced this throughout the centuries is through a practice known as lectio divina, which means divine reading. In lectio divina, we start with a relatively short passage, and we read it several times slowly and prayerfully, opening our hearts to whatever the Spirit may be speaking to us. Between each reading, we pause in stillness, quieting our soul to hear afresh from God. Slowing down in this way can heighten our ability to hear the Spirit speak to us from His Word.[13]

Let's practice this right now. Take a moment and ask the Holy Spirit to speak to you from His Word. Now slowly read the following (very familiar) passage a few times, pausing in stillness after each reading. Pay attention to anything in the passage that shimmers in your soul. What might God be saying to you in that?

"For God so loved the world that he gave his one and only Son, that whoever believes in him shall not perish but have eternal life" (John 3:16).

Don't rush this. Slowly read it five times. What is the Spirit saying to you? Write down what you are hearing.

The reason I chose a familiar passage is because I wanted us to see how slowing down in a passage—even a familiar one— can enable our hearts to hear things we wouldn't have heard otherwise.

Another creative way to practice Scripture meditation is to picture in your mind what this passage is describing. As we discussed in week one, this helps engage the right side of your brain so that you experience this truth more deeply.

What if, for example, as you are reading about Jesus calming the storm, you place yourself in that story? What if you feel the boat swaying back and forth, wondering how you will survive? What thoughts arise as you see Jesus sleeping? What emotions do you feel as He says to the storm, "Be still!" (Mark 4:39)?

Do you see how some intentional slowing down on our part can help make a passage come alive?

In Scripture meditation, we read slowly with an attentive mind and heart, being open to whatever God might want to say to us. Some days, something will shimmer. Other times, nothing will stand out to us. That's okay. This is not a sprint. It's a journey.

5. Write down what you are hearing God speak to you from His Word.

I encourage you to have a journal with you as you engage in Scripture meditation. Take a few moments to write down whatever you sense God saying to you from the passage you are reading. This enables you the opportunity to periodically review the things God has been speaking to your heart. One person I know uses his sabbath practice (more on that later) to take time to review what God has been speaking to his heart that week.

Imagine the impact over months and years of regularly opening your heart and mind to God's Word, allowing Him to speak to you and to sow seeds of life and truth in your heart. Your intimacy with Him will deepen because you are getting to know His heart. You are getting to know His Son.

Just like those two confused and discouraged followers of Jesus on the road to Emmaus, we can experience a renewal of hope and joy as Jesus opens the Scriptures to us.

This week in your exercises, you are going to combine the practices of stillness and prayer with the practice of Scripture meditation. For each exercise, I have chosen a different genre of Scripture so that you can practice meditating on varying types of passages. Again, the key is to read slowly and prayerfully, letting God speak to you from the passage. Have fun as you practice stillness, prayer, and Scripture meditation!

Exercises

EXERCISE ONE

Stillness
Begin with the practice of stillness (spiritual breathing, being present to your heart, being present to the Lord.)

Prayer
Pray through the Lord's Prayer (Presence, Praise, Purpose, Provision, Pardon, Protection).

Scripture
Now ask the Holy Spirit to speak to you from His Word.

Today you will be reading from Psalm 3, which is a song/poem written by David at one of the lowest points of his life. His son Absalom had betrayed and humiliated him. David was fleeing for his life when he wrote this psalm.

Start reading Psalm 3 slowly and prayerfully. If any word or phrase stands out to you or "shimmers" in your soul, stop there and take some time to reflect on that.

Ask the Lord, *What are You saying to me in these words?*

As time allows, continue reading the entire psalm in this way. Feel free to read through it a few times.

Take one of the thoughts or truths you felt God speaking to you and write it in a journal. Then express it in a prayer to God.

EXERCISE TWO

Stillness
Begin by practicing stillness.

Prayer
Pray through the Lord's Prayer.

Scripture
Ask the Holy Spirit to speak to you from His Word.

Today you will be reading a passage from the gospel of Luke that describes an encounter Jesus had with a man with leprosy. This is not a long passage, which gives opportunity to slow down in the text and let God speak to you from it.

Slowly read Luke 5:12–16 three or four times.

What words, phrases, actions are standing out to you?

Now imagine yourself as the leper in the story. What are you feeling? What is Jesus' heart toward you?

Take a moment and pray into whatever God is speaking to you from this passage.

EXERCISE THREE

Stillness
Begin with a time of stillness.

Prayer
Pray through the Lord's Prayer, with your heart open to how the Lord is leading you in each area.

Scripture
Ask the Holy Spirit to speak to you from His Word.

Slowly and prayerfully begin reading Matthew 7 from Jesus' Sermon on the Mount. Don't worry about getting through the entire chapter. Read until something "shimmers" or stands out to you. Stop at that point and spend time reflecting on that.

What is God saying to you?

Write it down. Then express that in a prayer to God.

Recommended Resource for Further Explanation

Podcast with Tyler Staton discussing Lectio Divina (February
18, 2020, https://pattern-podcast.blubrry.net/2020/02/18/
lectio-divina-tyler-staton/)

WEEK SIX

Practicing the Presence of Jesus

Pause to Review

Up to this point in this journey, we have been intentionally building into our lives three core practices that facilitate a deeper connection with Jesus: stillness, prayer, and Scripture meditation. As we have seen, these three core spiritual practices fit well together.

I encourage you to let these three practices be the foundation of your devotional time with God. The exercises in the remaining two weeks will include all three practices as a way to build these into the rhythm of our life.

Take a moment to reflect:

- How are these three practices impacting your relationship with Jesus?

- Do you need to make any adjustments in terms of scheduling or priorities?

This Week

As we have been saying throughout this journey, the spiritual practices we are experiencing are not the goal. The goal is a deeper, delight-filled connection with Jesus.

I love how author John Mark Comer articulates this. He writes, "The end [goal of these practices] is life to the full with Jesus. The end is to spend every waking moment in the conscious enjoyment of Jesus' company, to spend our entire lives with the most loving, joyful, peaceful person to ever live."[14]

That's our goal. Life with Jesus. Every waking moment in the conscious enjoyment of Jesus' company. That's ultimately what intimacy with Jesus looks like. A continual experience of Jesus' presence.

While the spiritual practices we have learned so far provide a foundation for connection with Jesus, how can we broaden our experience of Jesus to permeate all the other moments of our lives? We do so by embracing a fourth spiritual experience: practicing the presence of God.

The Normal Christian Life

In John 15, Jesus uses a powerful analogy to describe what a normal Christian life looks like: "I am the vine; you are the branches. If you remain in me and I in you, you will bear much fruit; apart from me you can do nothing" (John 15:5).

This is such a simple and yet vivid analogy of how Jesus invites us to live our lives. It is a life of constant connection to Him, a *continual* union with Him. A branch doesn't connect with the vine for a few minutes and then go out on its own the rest of the day. It would dry up. A branch's ability to bear fruit is completely dependent upon its continual connection to the vine.

This is the life Jesus longs for you and me to experience. This is the normal Christian life. Jesus urges us to "remain" in Him, continually staying connected to His presence.

Which sounds great, but how do we do this? How do we stay connected to Jesus in the midst of our everyday lives that are filled with working, running errands, shopping, cooking meals, doing homework, exercising, meeting with people, taking our car in for an oil change, going to the dentist . . . seriously? How is this possible?

Life is incredibly busy, and the bulk of that is doing things that don't feel very spiritual, things that don't help us feel very connected to Jesus. So how do we grow in this experience of remaining in Jesus? It ultimately boils down to one critical issue.

Awareness.

This is what makes the difference between us remaining in Christ or not. It is our awareness of Him. We find a fascinating example of this truth in Genesis 28 as Jacob is fleeing from his angry brother, Esau. While sleeping one evening, Jacob has a vivid dream of a stairway to heaven, and he hears God give to him an amazing promise.

When he wakes up from this experience, Jacob has this thought: "Surely the LORD is in this place, and I was not aware of it" (Genesis 28:16). What a fascinating statement. Jacob acknowledges that God was in that same place, but Jacob was not *aware* of His presence.

This wasn't about God showing up. God was already there. This was about Jacob's awareness of God's presence. Jacob wasn't tuning in to the God who was already there.

Isn't this so often how we live our lives? The Bible tells us that the presence of Jesus is with us wherever we go. The problem is, we are not consciously aware of His presence. We're not tuning in to this reality. In other words, we're not remaining in Him.

To remain in Christ has nothing to do with Him. It's all on our end. He is available. He is with us. The key is our learning how to cultivate a life in which we are increasingly aware of Jesus' presence with us no matter what we are doing.

Cultivating Our Awareness of Jesus

Part of our struggle is that we tend to view the various activities of our lives through a lens of "spiritual" or "not spiritual." If we're in church or listening to a worship song, that feels spiritual. But if we're washing our car or getting a haircut or teaching math or doing our rounds as a nurse, or whatever, that doesn't feel spiritual.

But that's not the way Jesus wants us to view our lives. From Jesus' perspective, all of life is spiritual. Every part of our lives is spiritual, because Jesus is with us in every place. What makes an experience "spiritual" is our awareness of Jesus in that space. This means that no matter what we are doing, we can experience it with Jesus as we intentionally cultivate our awareness of His presence with us.

One of the most impactful examples of living this kind of life was a man named Brother Lawrence, who lived in the seventeenth century. He was not well-educated, nor was he well-known. His life had been filled with suffering. As a young man, he served as a soldier but was seriously injured in battle. He later tried to be a footman but was too clumsy and awkward.

So, at the age of fifty-five, he joined a monastery and spent his life doing simple tasks of service, like washing dishes and clothing. He had no position of power or influence in the monastery. What he did possess, however, was a uniquely attractive relationship with Jesus. As people asked him questions about this, he articulated his thoughts in some personal correspondence. After his death, these letters were published and became a spiritual classic, read by millions of people.

In these letters, Brother Lawrence described in practical detail how he intentionally cultivated an awareness of Jesus' presence throughout his day.

Conversational Prayer

One of the ways Brother Lawrence cultivated this awareness of Jesus was through the practice of conversational prayer. In a correspondence with a friend, he described how we "can establish ourselves in a sense of the presence of God by continually talking to Him."[15]

Brother Lawrence intentionally cultivated a conversational prayer life with God throughout his day. Whether he was walking somewhere or washing dishes . . . didn't matter. His heart would be attuned to God's presence through prayer.

A very practical way to cultivate an abiding relationship with Jesus involves having an ongoing dialogue with Him throughout our day. In 1 Thessalonians 5:17, Paul urges us to "pray continually."

How do we do that? Paul cannot be talking about a life in which we stay in our room and pray all day. He's talking about a life in which we are in continual dialogue with Jesus about whatever is happening. When we are stuck on a problem at work, when we are in the middle of a difficult conversation, when we are sitting at a stoplight . . . we can pray.

Conversational prayer is a tangible way to turn our awareness toward God and to remain in His presence. The more we do this throughout the day, the more aware of Jesus' presence we become. It opens a door for Him to speak to our hearts, to give us wisdom or strength.

Whenever I am going into a difficult meeting or am feeling stuck in preparing a sermon or am walking down a hospital hallway to visit someone battling cancer and don't know what to say, I am often praying in that moment. *God help me. Spirit, fill me. I look to You.*

These "little" prayers can become a tangible way for us to practice the presence of Jesus throughout our day, inviting Him into every situation. This is not a substitute for our time alone with Him in our practices of stillness, prayer, and Scripture meditation. Those core spiritual practices provide a foundation for us to then cultivate a life of practicing the presence of Jesus throughout our day.

Another way to cultivate a life of conversational prayer is through a centuries-old practice known as simple prayer. In simple prayer, we take a simple phrase from the Bible, and we prayerfully repeat it. In doing so, it becomes a prayer that engages our heart.

The most historically well-known of these is adapted from a passage in Luke 18:13: "Lord Jesus Christ, have mercy on me, a sinner." Other scriptural simple prayers include "Your kingdom come" or "Help me overcome my unbelief."[16]

Some people attach these simple prayers to their breathing, as we explored in the practice of stillness. On the inhale, we can whisper, "Abba Father," and on the exhale, "I belong to You." Or (inhale) "Lord Jesus Christ" then (exhale) "have mercy on me, a sinner."

What makes simple prayer so powerful is its accessibility. We can utilize it anytime, anywhere. As we take a few seconds to repeat a simple prayer to the Lord, we are allowing our heart to be more aware of Jesus' presence with us.

Why don't you try this right now? Take a few moments and recite a few times the prayer, "Lord Jesus Christ, have mercy on me, a sinner."

How was that experience?

Delight Pause

In addition to conversational prayer, Brother Lawrence also discusses in his letters how throughout his day he would intentionally turn his mind toward God and simply enjoy God's love for him.

I call this a "delight pause." A delight pause occurs when we choose to stop in the midst of a busy day, and we take a few moments to open our heart to the reality of God's love for us. As we talked about in week one, experiencing the Lord's delight in us is the foundation for our life with Him. But rather than only practicing this in our devotional times with God, what if we stopped periodically throughout our day and let our soul experience afresh His delight in us?

When I take a delight pause, I may envision Jesus in front of me with a smile on His face, arms open wide. I take that moment to enjoy the Lord and to savor His love for me.

Savor.

That's not a word we use often enough. To savor is to slow down and enjoy something. Do you ever stop and look at the sunset and in that moment utter a prayer of praise and thanksgiving to God? Do you ever stop and savor a moment with a friend or a great cup of coffee or when someone has complimented you on something?

What if in those moments we stopped to savor that experience . . . in the Lord's presence, enjoying the blessing and thanking Him for it? What if we took a moment and simply expressed to Jesus our love for Him? *Jesus, I love You.*

These experiences of conversational prayer and delight pauses are practical ways to practice remaining in Jesus throughout our day. We are attuning our awareness to His presence in that moment.

Heart Access

Let me mention one other God-given opportunity that happens to us multiple times a day and provides a tangible way to practice Jesus' presence. Our emotions. Our emotions are a God-given opportunity to experience Jesus more deeply.

Unfortunately, the message we often hear, especially in Christian circles, is that negative emotions are bad and need to be replaced, resisted, or ignored. *You shouldn't feel angry or hurt or discouraged. You need to replace that with the joy of the Lord.*

While I do agree that joy is something we can cultivate, I also have found that our negative emotions are often beautiful opportunities to experience Jesus more deeply . . . if we choose to *explore* our emotions rather than *ignore* our emotions.

Our hearts are important to God. They become sacred space in which we experience intimacy with Him.

We see this on display in the first few pages of the Bible. In Genesis 4, Cain is ticked off because God accepted his brother Abel's sacrifice but not his. It is the first example of anger we see in the Bible. What's fascinating in this passage is *how* God approaches Cain in his anger.

God doesn't say, "Stop it, Cain. Let it go. Resist it." Nope. Instead, God asks Cain a question. "Why are you angry?" (Genesis 4:6). God wants Cain to *explore* his anger. His anger provides an opportunity to look into his heart and to welcome the truth and presence of God into that place.

I find this so amazing. In this passage, we see one of humanity's first post-fall interactions with God, and God instinctively assumes the posture of a skilled counselor. God is urging Cain to see his emotions as an opportunity to experience Him more deeply.

What if anytime we experienced a negative emotion during a day, we paused to ask ourselves this same question: *Why am I feeling this? Why am I feeling angry? Why am I feeling hurt? Why am I feeling afraid?* And then we let Jesus speak to us in that place.

I have noticed in my own life that my perfectionism (or Enneagram type 1, for you Enneagrammers) often results in feeling anger toward other people who aren't doing something the way I think it should be done. Sometimes I try to ignore it or stuff it.

But when I choose to stop and explore with Jesus my anger, I often see how my anger is really about my own reputation, or my own self-centeredness, or maybe my own fear of failure. Often underneath my anger is a lie I am believing: that I need to please people in order to feel good about myself, or that I need to be right in order for life to work. Other times, Jesus helps me realize that lie is rooted in a wounded place in my heart, and His love is the antidote.

Do you see how stopping to explore our negative emotions opens a beautiful door for us to experience life *with* Jesus?

What I love about this is that it fosters a compassionate approach toward ourselves and our negative emotions rather than a combative, shame-filled resistance that's often subtly encouraged in the church: *Just stop it. Stop feeling that way.* How freeing to realize that every negative emotion we experience becomes a place to practice the presence of Jesus—and in doing so, to become a healthier, more whole-hearted person.

When we make it our goal to resist or ignore these negative emotions, we are actually disconnecting from our hearts, which, as we learned earlier, is the very place God wants to meet us.

While this idea of exploring our negative emotions may be counterintuitive or difficult for many Christians, it is rooted in Scripture. This is how the Jewish people experienced God—with their whole hearts, even the negative parts.

Check out the brutal honesty of the psalmist:

As the deer pants for streams of water, so my soul pants for you, my God. My soul thirsts for God, for the living God. When can I go and meet with God? My tears have been my food day and night, while people say to me all day long, "Where is your God?" These things I remember as I pour out my soul: how I used to go to the house of God under the protection of the Mighty One with shouts of joy and praise, among the festive throng. (Psalm 42:1–4)

This guy is not ignoring his negative emotions. He is very present to them. Sadness, grief, disillusionment, heartache, anger, disappointment. But he doesn't stop there. He then explores these emotions. "Why, my soul, are you downcast? Why so disturbed within me?" (Psalm 42:5). There's that question again. *Why?*

He is exploring his own soul, welcoming the wisdom and presence of God into this place of discouragement and frustration. In that place, his heart receives a fresh truth from God.

Put your hope in God, for I will yet praise him, my Savior and my God. My soul is downcast within me; therefore I will remember you . . . By day the LORD directs his love, at night his song is with me—a prayer to the God of my life. (Psalm 42:5–8)

He is reminded of the Lord's love being poured out upon him day and night. I'm so glad the psalmist didn't try to resist or ignore his heart. He provides a beautiful example for us of what can happen when we take the time to explore our negative emotions.

We experience Jesus in that place.

Think of all the opportunities you and I have throughout a typical day to practice the presence of Jesus, to be aware of His Spirit, to welcome Him into every situation, including the negative emotions we feel.

Now, sometimes when I talk about this with people, they internally view practicing the presence of Jesus through a binary, pass/fail lens. Anything less than 100 percent awareness of Jesus throughout a typical day is failure. That's not very motivating.

But what if we changed the way we measure this? For example, what if we started at zero instead and made it our goal to consciously think of Jesus at least once every hour of our waking day. At the end of the day, we could estimate the number of times in which this happened. Anything above zero is a win! Once this becomes habit, we could begin to shorten the interval—from one hour to every half hour, etc.[17]

Let's not make 100 percent awareness our goal. That's unachievable and discouraging. What if we simply made our goal a *greater* awareness of Jesus' presence than we are currently experiencing in our lives? That would mean we are growing in our experience of life with Jesus. How cool is that?

Exercises

Each day's exercise this week includes the spiritual practices of stillness, prayer, and Scripture meditation, as well as an activity to practice the presence of Jesus throughout that day.

EXERCISE ONE

Stillness

Begin with a time of stillness (as we have been practicing in previous weeks. Be present to your heart and mind).

Prayer

Pray through the Lord's Prayer.

Scripture

Slowly and prayerfully read John 15:1–5. What words, phrases, verses shimmer for you? Ask the Lord what He is saying to you in this passage.

Practicing His Presence

Now ask the Lord to help you be more aware of His presence throughout your day. Intentionally take a few delight pauses today, where you stop for a minute or two and enjoy the Lord delighting in you. Consider setting an alarm on your phone as a reminder.

EXERCISE TWO

Stillness

Spend a few minutes in the practice of stillness. Tune in to your heart. Where are you, really? What parts of you are needing to be noticed?

Prayer

Pray through the Lord's Prayer.

Scripture

Ask the Holy Spirit to speak to you. Slowly and prayerfully meditate on Psalm 73.

Reflect on the psalmist's emotional journey in this psalm. What is his heart initially feeling? Where does his heart end up? What changed?

Take some time to be present to your heart by identifying a negative emotion you are feeling.

Explore that emotion with the Lord. Ask the Lord, *Why am I feeling this?*

What does He want to say to you in the midst of that emotion?

Practicing His Presence

Throughout the next twenty-four hours, cultivate a conversational relationship with Him throughout your day. Is there anything He wants to whisper to your heart?

EXERCISE THREE

Reflect on the previous twenty-four hours. Were there any moments you intentionally tuned in to the presence of God? Did He whisper anything to your heart?

Stillness

Spend a few minutes practicing stillness. Is there a question you are wanting to ask the Lord?

Prayer

Pray through the Lord's Prayer.

Scripture

Slowly and prayerfully read Psalm 23.

What words, phrases, thoughts are shimmering for you? What is the Lord saying to you? Turn that into a prayer to Him.

Practicing His Presence

At various times over the next twenty-four hours, practice praying the simple prayer, "Lord Jesus Christ, have mercy on me, a sinner." Be aware of Jesus' presence with you.

Recommended Resources for Further Exploration

The Practice of the Presence of God: A 40-Day Devotion Based on Brother Lawrence's The Practice of the Presence of God by Brother Lawrence and Alan Vermilye

Present Perfect: Finding God in the Now by Gregory A. Boyd

Simple Prayer: Learning to Speak to God with Ease by Charlie Dawes

WEEK SEVEN

Sabbath

Pause to Review

Take a moment to reflect:

- How was your experience of practicing the presence of Jesus this past week?

- Which of the suggested tools (conversational prayer, simple prayer, delight pauses, exploring our emotions) did you find most helpful?

This Week

Now, we will explore together a fifth and our final core spiritual practice that is vital to our spiritual health and our intimacy with Jesus—the practice of Sabbath. This practice is a very prominent theme throughout Scripture, and yet it is something that many Christ followers struggle to understand and to experience.

Let's be honest. The idea of Sabbath feels so . . . I don't know . . . Old Testament? Archaic? Irrelevant? For many of us, it feels light years removed from our reality. But is it? As followers of Jesus, we probably ought to begin by acknowledging an obvious but significant truth.

Jesus, our Savior and Lord, practiced Sabbath.

Now, granted, often His practice of Sabbath ticked off the religious leaders, resulting in an exasperated reaction from Jesus. But Sabbath was an integral part of Jesus' life. His continual frustration around this practice was not that the Jewish leaders practiced Sabbath but *how* they practiced Sabbath. In their practice of Sabbath, they had missed the heart of the Sabbath.

The Heart of Sabbath

In order to understand the heart of Sabbath, we need to start at the beginning . . . literally. In Genesis 1 we see God creating the heavens and the earth and filling the earth with living creatures. The rhythm of this passage involves six days of creating.

> God saw all that he had made, and it was very good. And there was evening, and there was morning—the sixth day. Thus the heavens and the earth were completed in all their vast array. By the seventh day God had finished the work he had been doing; so on the seventh day he rested from all his work. Then God blessed the seventh day and made it holy, because on it he rested from all the work of creating that he had done. (Genesis 1:31–2:3)

How amazing to realize that God Himself rested. In His very being and activity, God affirmed both the value of work and the value of rest. He set aside one day out of seven for the purpose of physical rest.

But there's more.

Notice how God views the Sabbath: "Then God blessed the seventh day and made it holy" (Genesis 2:3). From the beginning, we see the significance of Sabbath in God's purposes and plans. There is blessing in it. It is a sacred, holy thing.

So, it's no surprise that much later, when God rescues His people from slavery in Egypt, He says to them,

> Remember the Sabbath day by keeping it holy. Six days you shall labor and do all your work, but the seventh day is a sabbath to the LORD your God. On it you shall not do any work . . . Therefore the LORD blessed the Sabbath day and made it holy. (Exodus 20:8–11)

This Sabbath command is included here as part of the Ten Commandments, which are the core practices God established to protect and provide for His people. You know, things like, you shall not murder, you shall not worship other gods, and also, remember to honor the Sabbath. What? How did Sabbath make this list?

Clearly, this is a big deal. The practice of Sabbath is not some archaic, outdated idea. Nor is it some optional, insignificant thing. God wants us to practice Sabbath. But why? God tells us exactly why. In both Genesis 2 and Exodus 20 we see this repeated idea: "Therefore the LORD blessed the Sabbath day and made it holy" (Exodus 20:11).

Those two words—*blessed* and *holy*—are crucial in our understanding of the purpose of the Sabbath.

The Blessing of Sabbath

What does it mean that God *blessed* the Sabbath day? It means there is blessing for us in our practicing Sabbath. The Sabbath is a gift to those who practice it. It is a place of life and blessing.

The word *Sabbath* literally means "to cease from." The idea of Sabbath is that one day in seven, we cease from what we have been doing the other six days.

We cease from working.
We cease from producing.
We cease from hurrying.
We cease from doing our chores and our to-do lists.
We cease from responding to work-related emails.
We cease from running from one meeting or activity to the next.

And in that ceasing from, we have now created space . . . margin . . . to simply be. To rest. To slow down. To restore our souls. Doesn't that sound wonderful?

Sabbath is an incredible gift from God—a day in which we don't have to produce anything. It is the gift of being reminded of our true identity. Author A. J. Swoboda writes, "Sabbath is a scheduled weekly reminder that we are not what we do; rather we are who we are loved by."[18]

Sabbath is also this much-needed reminder at the core of our being that we are not in control of the universe. God is. Isn't it interesting how the universe keeps going even when we stop for twenty-four hours? But so often we live as if it all depends on us. Sabbath is a regular reminder to our soul that it doesn't all depend on us.

Theologian Abraham Joshua Heschel, in his book *The Sabbath*, invites us to "rest on the Sabbath as if all your work were done."[19] And I would add, *because in Christ it is done.* Sabbath is not simply an Old Testament concept. It is a gospel reality. Sabbath is a day to be reminded of the life-changing truth Jesus shouted from the cross: "It is finished."

Sabbath is one day out of seven in which we are invited to live without the to-do list hanging over our head. I don't know about you, but I'm a "to-do list" person. Even on a day off, I have a list of things to do, items to accomplish. It makes me nervous to have a space of time with no to-do list or action plan.

Why is that?

Why does my anxiety level rise when I remove the to-do list? Could it be that I am addicted to being productive because productivity is where I find value? If someone asks me, "How was your day?" my answer to that question depends on how much I got done that day.

In our driven, busy, hurried, distracted culture, Sabbath is a radical idea. Dr. Walter Brueggemann describes Sabbath as an act of resistance.[20] The practice of Sabbath is an insurgency and insurrection against our culture's idolatry of productivity and materialism. Sabbath is an unsettling idea for many of us who live on the adrenaline of hurry and busyness and activity.

Which is why we need it.

From the beginning, God knew that we would tend to measure our value and worth according to what we do and how much we produce. This inevitably leads to a life of hurry and constant activity, which takes a toll on our soul. Sabbath is a divinely ordered detox for us, helping us break free from our addiction to doing.

Sabbath provides the gift of saying no to producing, the gift of slowing down, the gift of rest.

Again, this is the blessing of Sabbath. It is something that our soul, our relationships, our physical bodies desperately need . . . and yet it is not something we naturally make time for.

When is the last time you carved out twenty-four hours and, in that time, didn't produce anything, check work emails, run errands, or go shopping? I'm guessing that for many of us, it's probably been a long time.

What kind of impact is this having in our lives?

Sabbath Is Holy

Not only is the purpose of Sabbath to bring blessing into our lives. We are told in Exodus 20:8 that God made the Sabbath "holy." It is fascinating to realize that this is the very first thing in creation that God calls holy—not a place, like a mountain or a temple. Out of his whole creation, the first thing God calls holy is a period of time.

Our experiencing Sabbath is a holy thing.

So, what does that mean? The word *holy* means set apart for God. Sabbath is a day we set aside to be present to God, to worship Him, to reflect on His goodness, to enjoy Him.

Earlier I mentioned that the word *Sabbath* means "to cease from." The word *Sabbath* can also mean "to delight in." It possesses this dual idea of ceasing from something in order to experience something else, creating margin so that we have time to fill our souls afresh with God.

Sabbath is not simply a day off. It is a day set aside to be present with God. To worship Him. To enjoy His delight in us. To experience His creation. To reflect on His blessings in our lives.

In his Sabbath command to us, God is saying, *"I want you to take one day a week, and on that day, I want you to slow down, to reflect on your life, to enjoy creation and relationships. Let My presence fill and refresh your soul. Take time to ponder, to worship, to reflect, and to enjoy."*

Can you imagine actually seeing a sunset happen rather than a passing glance out the rearview mirror as you hurry to another event? What if God is the event? What if time isn't a commodity to be maximized but a gift to enjoy in that moment?

This is the gift that Sabbath is to us and to our souls—the gift of ceasing from the pressures and stresses of life in order to delight in the only One who can truly satisfy our souls.

Let's be honest. Our lives are so busy, so stressful, so complex. In the practice of Sabbath, God invites us to take time to root our souls in simplicity. To slow down, to stop producing, to be reminded that our identity is in God, and to find our life and enjoyment in Him and His blessings.

Sabbath is an opportunity to engage in things that pour life into us. To go on a hike. To take a nap. To connect with a friend. To read a book we've been wanting to read. To dream. To reflect on the past week. To savor.

There is no to-do list. It's a day to enjoy, a day to be.

The How of Sabbath

Now that we have looked at the *why* of Sabbath, let's talk about the *how* of Sabbath. What are some logistics of practicing Sabbath?

Before we go there, let's agree that we are going to steer clear of anything that even hints at making the same mistake the Pharisees made regarding Sabbath-keeping. They were so intent on helping people keep the Sabbath that they created over six hundred man-made regulations—things you could and couldn't do on the Sabbath. For instance, you couldn't look in the mirror on the Sabbath. They were concerned that if you noticed a gray hair, you might pull it out, which would be "work." Better to avoid looking into a mirror altogether, so they thought.

I'm sure each of these Sabbath-keeping tips were attempts to help people practice Sabbath, but sadly, the result was an exhausting "banned behavior" list that became a burden for people. Remember, the Sabbath is supposed to be a gift to us. Unfortunately, all their rules turned it into a legalistic set of things to avoid. They took the joy and life out of the gift God had given.

We don't want to do that. We don't want to create a new "Christianized" version of Sabbath dos and don'ts. But we do want to take this command seriously.

So, what does that look like? It looks like carving out twenty-four hours in our weekly rhythm and in that time intentionally ceasing from so many of the things we have filled our other six days with—working, shopping, producing, studying, hurrying, list keeping, etc.

Instead, we choose to rest. We choose to spend time enjoying the Lord and enjoying relationships and enjoying things that replenish us and pour life into our soul.

Another way to say this is that Sabbath is a day where we remove our "ought to" list:

I *ought* to get up early. Then don't get up early.

I *ought* to exercise. Then don't exercise.

I *ought* to mow the lawn. I *ought* to weed the garden. I *ought* to go shopping. I *ought* to fix that broken cabinet. Then don't . . . you get the idea.

We have spent the other six days doing our ought-to list. Sabbath is a day we intentionally free ourselves from "oughts."

Now, if you have young children, I'm not talking about ignoring them for twenty-four hours (no matter how tempting that sounds). You must figure out what Sabbath looks like in your season of life. Maybe for you Sabbath is having someone watch your kids for a few hours and you doing something you want to do (not grocery shopping). If you are in that stage of life, give yourself grace in trying to figure out ways to experience Sabbath together as a family.

I remember when our children were young, my wife Raylene and I designated Sunday afternoons as nap time for everyone. We turned off all electronics, and each family member either read a book or took a nap. I know of families who do a family night on their Sabbath, cooking a fun meal together and playing games.

That's the wonderful thing about Sabbath. You can be creative and make it personal. What pours life into you? What things would you enjoy? What places or spaces would pour into your relationship with God? What is that thing that if you did it during the week, you'd feel guilty about wasting time?

Sabbath is an invitation to guilt-free "time wasting."

But of course, it is not a waste of time. It is an investment into our soul, our relationship with God, and our emotional and spiritual health. So, for example, if mowing the lawn or cooking is life-giving and fun for you, feel free to do that on your Sabbath. But if those things are an obligation, then plan ahead so that you don't have to mow the lawn or cook on that day.

Some Practical Suggestions

Here are a few other suggestions you might find helpful in this practice.

1. Remember that the Sabbath time period does not have to start at midnight.

In Jewish culture, Sabbath started in the evening. You might find it helpful to do the same. A family could start their Sabbath with a family dinner on a Saturday evening, leading into a game night with their kids, sleeping in the next morning, going to a late morning worship service, relaxing in the afternoon, and then ending the Sabbath at dinner.

I personally like that rhythm of starting Sabbath in the evening, because it helps me ease into Sabbath at the end of a busy day. But again, this is just a suggestion.

2. If you have a family, plan your Sabbath together.

If you are married, plan your Sabbath together with your spouse so that both of you experience a Sabbath that is life-giving. Let's try to avoid any communication that sounds like, "Hey dear, I'm headed to the golf course for my Sabbath. Have fun with the kids." Help your spouse experience Sabbath as well. If that means helping shop or cook ahead of time, great.

If you have teenagers at home, include them in this practice. What a great discipleship opportunity for them to grow in—to learn how to take a break from technology, to slow down, and to tune in to their hearts.

3. The Sabbath can be any day of the week.

I realize that certain groups make a big deal about how the Sabbath must be practiced on a particular day. What we see in Scripture is that for the Jews, Saturday was their Sabbath. But after Jesus rose again on Sunday, Christians began observing Sabbath on Sunday.

All of this shows us that the actual day is not a crucial issue. The crucial issue is figuring out how, in the midst of our own personal schedule, we can carve out a twenty-four-hour period for rest, for the Lord, for reflection, for slowing down, for not working.

———

In our technologically driven culture where we are continually attached to work, to technology, etc., Sabbath is a radical, countercultural decision. So it won't be easy. But it will be worth it. God promises His blessing in it.

That is a great reminder for me. Even though I regularly teach on the importance of Sabbath, and I wholeheartedly believe in the blessing and benefit of Sabbath, I still often struggle to carve out a twenty-four-hour period of time for this myself. It feels weird to say, but the practice of Sabbath is a continual battle for me, which is a vivid reminder of why I need it.

Practicing Sabbath This Week

One of our exercises this week is to carve out twenty-four hours to experience what we have been talking about. If that seems unattainable, feel free to start where you are. Maybe three hours or six hours. That would be a great place to begin, with the goal being a full twenty-four hours.

One more thing: Be ready for the guilt trip. Be ready for that feeling on your Sabbath that you ought to be doing something productive. Resist that idea. There will be time to do those other things, six days of time, in fact. The Sabbath is a gift to you. So, this week, let's make time for this gift and enjoy it!

Exercises

This week there will be three regular exercises involving stillness, prayer, Scripture meditation, and practicing the presence of Jesus, plus a fourth exercise involving you scheduling and experiencing a Sabbath.

EXERCISE ONE

Stillness

Spend some time in stillness, being present to your heart and mind. Where are you, really?

Now take a few moments to enjoy the Lord's presence with you. Feel free to imagine Jesus standing in front of you, with His arms open wide to you. Is there any question you want to ask Him?

Prayer

Spend time praying through the Lord's Prayer, being attentive to the Spirit's promptings.

Scripture

Slowly read and meditate on Isaiah 58:13–14.

What longings are being stirred in you for your Sabbath practice?

Practicing His Presence

Make it your goal today to think of Jesus at least once every waking hour.

EXERCISE TWO

Stillness

Spend time practicing stillness, bringing your whole self before God. Take time to tune in to your heart. What emotions are you experiencing today? Welcome the Lord into those places.

Prayer

Spend time praying through the Lord's Prayer, being attentive to the Spirit's promptings.

Scripture

Slowly and prayerfully read Mark 2:23–3:6.

What is God saying to you in this passage?

What concerns do you have about practicing Sabbath? Share those with the Lord.

Practicing His Presence

In the midst of your day today, intentionally stop to enjoy a delight pause. Enjoy the Father's love for you.

EXERCISE THREE

Stillness
Spend time practicing stillness, being present to your heart. Now be present to the Lord. Enjoy His love for you.

Prayer
Now pray through the sections of the Lord's Prayer. If you don't get through all of them, that's totally fine. Be aware of how the Spirit is leading you in your prayer time with Him.

Scripture
Slowly and prayerfully read Matthew 11:28–30. Imagine Jesus speaking these words directly to you. What burdens are you carrying? Imagine yourself releasing to Jesus each of those specific burdens.

Now ask Jesus what He wants to give you in exchange. What does He give you?

Practicing His Presence
Throughout your day today, intentionally enjoy a conversational dialogue with Jesus. Welcome Him into situations you wouldn't normally think of doing so.

SABBATH EXERCISE

Schedule and experience a Sabbath. No shoulds, no oughts, no work-related emails, no to-do list. What does your heart want to do? Take time to do that. Enjoy yourself. Enjoy the Lord.

After your Sabbath experience, spend some time reflecting on the experience by answering the following questions:

What was meaningful for you during your Sabbath?

What was frustrating or challenging for you during your Sabbath?

Recommended Resources for Further Exploration

The Rest of God: Restoring Your Soul by Restoring Sabbath by Mark Buchanan

Subversive Sabbath: The Surprising Power of Rest in a Nonstop World by A. J. Swoboda

"Six Ways to Practice the Sabbath" by Tim Keller (Redeemer.com, March 2018, https://www.redeemer.com/redeemer-report/article/six_ways_to_practice_sabbath)

NEXT STEPS

How to Keep the Momentum Going

For the past seven weeks, you have been intentionally building into your life five core spiritual practices that are opening the door for deeper connection with Jesus. You have momentum. Cool things are happening.

The crucial question is, How do you keep that momentum going? By choosing to *continue* to engage in these practices, building them into the rhythm of your life.

Scientific research has shown that, in terms of habit formation, it takes sixty-six days to establish a habit in our lives. We start out in the "honeymoon" phase where we are motivated and energized. Everything feels great.

But this inevitably leads to the "fight through" phase. In this phase, we don't feel as motivated. It's hard to get up early, hard to carve out our Sabbath space, hard to practice stillness. The practices become more of a struggle, requiring a decision to keep going. Maybe you have already experienced this in your journey so far.

But here's the cool thing. When we choose to fight through that natural resistance, we eventually end up in the "second nature" phase, where these things are now a normal part of our lives. If we miss a few days, we notice. We feel it and are motivated to get back on track.

That's what we want.

We want these spiritual practices to become a normal, essential part of our life so that if we start to miss them, we notice. We notice how we are starting to feel edgy, frustrated, stressed. We realize how much we miss those times of stillness with Jesus where we were being present to our heart. We long for a Sabbath experience in the midst of our busy lives . . . and we choose to get back on track. We choose to re-engage in these practices that we know are life-giving to our soul.

A Rule of Life

In his book *The Relentless Elimination of Hurry*, John Mark Comer introduces a helpful and historically rooted concept known as a rule of life.[21] After the initial explosion of vibrant Christianity in the first few centuries, many Christian leaders were seduced by political power and money. Ornate cathedrals were built, but there was a lack of holiness and humility, a lack of simple intimacy with Jesus. The church became rife with corruption. Spiritually speaking, it truly was the Dark Ages.

During this time, there were groups of Christ followers deeply troubled by these realities. They didn't want to be seduced by these things, so they essentially removed themselves from society and created monastic orders where they could follow Jesus in community.

In each order, that community of faith would agree upon and commit to certain regular spiritual practices that would help them walk with Jesus. This commitment was known as a rule of life. This rule of life was an intentional way to *not* be shaped by the world but rather to be shaped by the Lord.

When I look at our society today and how easily we as believers are being shaped and formed by it, I believe this idea of a rule of life can be a very strategic thing for our spiritual lives.

What if we committed ourselves to these five core practices of stillness, prayer, Scripture meditation, practicing the presence of Jesus, and Sabbath as an intentional way to allow ourselves to be shaped and formed by Jesus rather than by the world around us?

That decision would have a significant impact in our lives. I heard someone recently say, "One Sabbath won't change your life, but a lifetime of Sabbaths might save it." That's true with all the practices we have experienced in this journey.

You have been practicing these things for a few weeks, so they are already becoming a part of your rule of life. Let's keep that momentum going!

Some Practical Suggestions

As you are thinking through your next steps, let me offer a few practical suggestions.

1. Join the practices of stillness, prayer, and Scripture meditation into one activity.

In my quiet times with the Lord (which I try to do four to five times a week), I combine these three core practices. I begin with stillness, then transition into prayer, and conclude with Scripture meditation. Feel free to change up the order, depending on what works best for you.[22]

As an example of how this might work, here's a resource our church put together a few years ago to help people build these three practices into the rhythm of their lives.

How to Spend Twenty Minutes with God

1. Stillness (4 minutes)

Begin with spiritual breathing—on the inhale say, "Spirit of God"; on the exhale say, "Breathe on me."

Be present to your inner being. What thoughts are filling your mind? What emotions are you feeling right now? Where are you, really?

Be present to the Lord. Imagine Jesus standing before you or sitting with you. Enjoy His presence with you.

2. Prayer (8 minutes)

Pray through the Lord's Prayer: Presence, Praise, Purpose, Provision, Pardon, and Protection.

3. Scripture (8 minutes)

Ask the Holy Spirit to speak to you from His Word.

Slowly read a passage of Scripture. If something "shimmers," stop there and reread it. What is God saying to you? Express that to Him in a prayer.

As you can see, this resource incorporates all three of these core spiritual practices into one experience, so that this can easily be built into the natural rhythm of your life. Don't get hung up on the "twenty minutes" descriptor. That is a general estimate. Some days it may be shorter than that. Other days, longer. The point is not the time length. The point is that we are consistently spending time with Jesus.

2. Embrace variety.

In each of the practices in this journey, I provided a basic template that has worked for me. But if you find yourself in a place where you are not connecting as well with a particular practice, feel free to change it up.

Perhaps change the Bible reading plan you are using. Pick a book in the Bible and go through it at your own pace. Pick a theme and look at Scriptures related to that theme. Or change Bible versions that you are using.

Maybe change the location of your time of stillness. Take a walk. Listen to some worship songs during that time. Perhaps change the way you are praying. Take a break from the Lord's Prayer to explore a different way of praying.

Spiritual formation is a journey. There may be seasons when these specific practices aren't feeding your soul the way they had previously. Sometimes we walk through dark valleys where we don't feel like we are connecting with God. In these places, we often feel like failures, like we're not doing something right. All of which is a complete lie. You are not alone. You are not going backward. You are not a failure.

Here's the truth: Every wall you hit, every valley you experience is a divine opportunity to go deeper in your relationship with God. Rather than *checking out*, choose to *lean in* to Jesus, to explore what Jesus is doing in your heart and life in that season.

Remember the goal—intimacy with Jesus. He wants to meet you where you are and in the way He has wired your personality. So feel free to embrace variety in these practices as you discover what connects with you in particular seasons.

3. Have companions on the journey.

Historically speaking, one of the most impactful aspects of the "rule of life" concept was that these people of faith decided to embrace this commitment *together*. They knew they needed each other to help resist being shaped by the negative aspects of the culture around them.

Are there people around you who would want to pursue this journey with you? Not only does this help keep us on track. It's also a lot more fun!

4. Make a plan.

Ultimately, this comes down to an intentional decision you and I must make to build these core practices into the rhythm of our lives. Take a couple minutes right now to think through the rule of life you desire to implement. What is your plan for each practice? Write your answer in the space provided.

- What is your plan for stillness, prayer, and Scripture meditation (when, where, how often, Bible reading plan, etc.)?

- What is your plan for practicing the presence of Jesus?

- What is your plan for practicing Sabbath?

Don't Forget . . .

I want to conclude by reminding us where we started in this journey: God delights in you! You are loved by a God who longs for deeper levels of intimacy with you. The spiritual practices are simply tools to intentionally help you move toward the loving heart of God.

I love how Henry Nouwen often described the purpose of these spiritual practices. They are to create space in our lives "to hear the voice of God call us 'my Beloved.'"[23]

That's the invitation from Jesus to you. May the Lord deepen your experience of intimacy with Him as you create space to hear Him call you "My Beloved."

APPENDIX

Small Group Study Guide

A crucial aspect of doing this as a group is the opportunity each week to talk about how the exercises went for each person. Without each person doing the exercises, the group simply becomes a discussion group. So, take some time your first week to agree to both read the content and do the exercises. Each week's questions will include time to talk about how the exercises went.

Week One: How Does God Feel About You?

1. In Zephaniah 3:17 and Numbers 6:24–26, we see the heart of God toward us—a loving parent delighting in and smiling toward His children. How fully do you *experience* God's love for you? Don't give the Sunday School answer (I know God loves me, etc.). The question is, How fully are you *experiencing* His love for you? Do you regularly *feel* His delight in you?

2. Paul talks in Romans 5:5 about the Holy Spirit being poured out into our hearts so that we can experience the lavish love of God the Father. What do you think keeps people from experiencing in their hearts this lavish love? Feel free to share from your own experience.

3. Romans 8:16 describes how the Spirit "testifies with our spirit that we are God's children." What does this "testifying" look and feel like in practical terms? How do we more fully experience this crucial ministry of the Spirit?

4. What is the potential long-term impact of pursuing a Christianity in which the love of the Father is never truly experienced in a person's heart?

5. Take some time to talk about how you did with the three exercises for this week. Were they helpful in you experiencing the Lord's love more deeply? Discuss.

6. In light of what you learned in this week's content, what are some practical ways you can experience the Father's love more deeply this coming week?

Week Two: Stillness

1. How would you summarize the purpose of practicing stillness?

2. Take a few minutes and talk about your experience of stillness in the exercises for this week. How was it? Easy? Difficult? Life-giving? Frustrating?

3. What are you finding are the biggest barriers to your experience of stillness? For each barrier, discuss a strategy to help you navigate that barrier.

4. How do you handle distractions that come to mind when you try to practice stillness?

5. Let's practice as a group. Take a minute or two of silence

to tune in to your heart. What emotions are you experiencing right now from the day? Feel free to use the S-H-A-D-E-S acronym (page 31). Now share with the group one or two of the things going on in your heart.

6. As you think about the practice of stillness becoming a part of your life, share with your group how you plan to create space for this, including the "where" and "when" of your plan.

Week Three: Listening to Jesus

1. What have been your past experiences in this area of listening to the voice of Jesus? Have they been positive, negative, or something else?

2. Take a few minutes to talk about how the exercises were for you this week. Did you feel like you heard Jesus' voice? Discuss.

3. What is the difference between hearing and listening? What are some things that are required in order to listen well to another person?

4. How does God most often whisper to your inner being? A thought, a word, a picture, a song, etc.? How attentive are you these days to that whisper?

5. What do you think of the idea of asking God specific questions and then listening to His response?

6. How do you personally try to discern whether what you are hearing is from God?

Week Four: Prayer

1. What is your biggest struggle or challenge in your experience of prayer?

2. How was your experience with the prayer exercises for this week?

3. What part or parts of the Lord's Prayer have already been a regular part of your prayer life, and which parts of the Lord's Prayer are a new addition?

4. When you think about praying "Your kingdom come" and partnering with God to bring His rule into certain situations or needs in our world, what specific areas of need come to mind?

5. Why do you think Jesus included in His prayer a regular opportunity not only to ask for forgiveness but to choose to forgive others? What specific impact might this have in our lives as we include it in our prayer experience?

Week Five: Engaging in Scripture

1. In your spiritual journey, what has been your personal experience with engaging with the Bible?

2. Read Psalm 1:1–4. What does it mean to "delight" in God's Word? What would cause a person to delight in Scripture?

3. Psalm 1 says that a person who meditates on the Word is like a tree planted by streams of water. Take some time to tease out this analogy. In what ways does meditation have this impact?

4. How was your practice of meditation in the exercises for this week? Share one specific thing that Jesus spoke to your heart from one of the passages you looked at.

Week Six: Practicing the Presence of Jesus

1. How was your experience of practicing the presence of Jesus this past week?

2. Which of the suggested tools most resonated with you—conversational prayer, simple prayer, delight pauses, or stopping to explore your emotions?

3. In Genesis 28:16, Jacob declares, "Surely the LORD is in this place, and I was not aware of it." Being *aware* of God's presence with us can make the most "nonspiritual" activity a "spiritual" activity. Think of an area or activity in your life that feels unspiritual. What would it look like to intentionally practice the presence of Jesus in that place?

4. Have someone in your group slowly read John 15:5 a few times. As you meditate on this verse, what stands out to you?

5. What would you expect to be some of the fruit of a life lived *with* Jesus, being aware of His presence throughout your day?

6. What specific steps will you take this week to grow in this area?

Week Seven: Sabbath

1. What has been your experience of Sabbath over the course of your Christian life? Overly rigid? Nonexistent? Hit-or-miss?

2. How was your experience of Sabbath this past week? Was it easy to do, or was it difficult? Explain.

3. What is your biggest obstacle in making the practice of Sabbath a regular part of your life?

4. How can we navigate the tension between the Sabbath being a gift to us and yet also being a struggle to implement into our lives?

5. What do you long to experience in your practice of Sabbath?

Next Steps: How to Keep the Momentum Going

1. What is your plan moving forward to build into your life these five core spiritual practices? Be specific.

2. How can this group help you in these next steps in your journey with Jesus?

Notes

1   John Mark Comer, "How We Change: Intentional Spiritual Formation," sermon at Bridgetown Church, Portland, Oregon, November 19, 2017, https://bridgetown.church/teachings/discovering-your-identity-calling/how-we-change-intentional-spiritual-formation.

2   Sociological and neuroscientific research affirms this relational reality. From the moment of birth, being delighted in fosters emotional health and a deepened capacity for relational attachment. The book *The Other Half of Church: Christian Community, Brain Science, and Overcoming Spiritual Stagnation* by Jim Wilder and Michel Hendricks (Chicago: Moody Publishers, 2020) explains this in more detail.

3   Maybe, like me, you were taught the "Fact, Faith, Feelings" train. Facts are the engine; our feelings are the caboose. The clear implication of that analogy is that, in our relationship with God, our heart is not as important as our head. In other words, we should not expect to feel God's love for us. But Paul often talked about us experiencing God's love (see Ephesians 3:16–19 and Romans 8:37–39).

4   Even though this practice is articulated throughout Scripture, some Christians are hesitant to utilize this out of concern that this feels New Age. But there is a key distinction between New Age visualization and biblical imaging. In biblical imaging, we are using Scripture to stir our imagination. We are envisioning a truth the Bible describes rather than visualizing whatever we want. Biblical imaging helps us experience the truths contained in Scripture. In other words, it is thoroughly biblical.

5   At our church, we have a ministry called Hope Abounds that focuses on this type of prayer work. Feel free to call Christ Community Church

in Greeley, Colorado, to make an appointment. Zoom meetings are an option for those who live out of the area.

6   Chuck DeGroat, *Wholeheartedness: Busyness, Exhaustion, and Healing the Divided Self* (Grand Rapids, MI: Eerdmans, 2016), 123.

7   DeGroat, 145.

8   John Eldredge, *Get Your Life Back: Everyday Practices for a World Gone Mad* (Nashville, TN: Nelson Books, 2020), 6.

9   For example, see John 1:38, John 14:9, and Luke 24:17, to name a few.

10   Alan Kraft, *More: When A Little Bit of the Spirit is Not Enough* (Greeley, CO: Joshua Luke Press, 2014), 80–81.

11   If you want more practical input into how to grow in this, I spend four chapters on this subject in my book *More: When a Little Bit of the Spirit Is Not Enough*.

12   You can find this prayer by searching online for "John Eldredge Daily Prayer" or at wildatheart.org as well as on their Wild at Heart app. At times I will listen to the audio version of this prayer on my way to work.

13   For a helpful description of lectio divina, check out this podcast interview with Pastor Tyler Staton: https://pattern-podcast.blubrry.net/2020/02/18/lectio-divina-tyler-staton/ (Pattern Podcast, February 18, 2020).

14   John Mark Comer, *The Ruthless Elimination of Hurry: How to Stay Emotionally Healthy and Spiritually Alive in the Chaos of the Modern World* (Colorado Springs, CO: WaterBrook, 2019), 107.

15   Brother Lawrence/Alan Vermilye, *The Practice of the Presence of God: A 40-Day Devotion based on Brother Lawrence's* The Practice of the Presence of God (Mount Juliet, TN: Brown Chair Books, 2021), 58.

16   Charles Dawes, *Simple Prayer: Learning to Speak to God with Ease* (Downers Grove, IL: InterVarsity Press, 2017), chapters 1 and 2.

17   For an example of someone pursuing this, see Frank Charles Laubach's brief book *The Game with Minutes*, in which he describes a game he created in which his goal is to think of Jesus at least one time every minute.

18   A. J. Swoboda, *Subversive Sabbath: The Surprising Power of Rest in a Nonstop World* (Grand Rapids, MI: Brazos Press, 2018), 17.

19 Abraham Joshua Heshel, *The Sabbath*, illustrated edition (New York City, New York: Farrar Straus Giroux, 2005), 32.

20 Walter Brueggemann, *Sabbath as Resistance: Saying No to the Culture of Now* (Louisville, KY: Westminster John Knox Press, 2017).

21 John Mark Comer, *The Ruthless Elimination of Hurry: How to Stay Emotionally Healthy and Spiritually Alive in the Chaos of the Modern World* (Colorado Springs, CO: WaterBrook, 2019), 93.

22 For many years, I started with Scripture, then the practice of stillness followed by prayer.

23 There are various places in which he used this language. For instance, see the January 13 entry in *Bread for the Journey: A Daybook of Wisdom and Faith* (New York: HarperOne, 1997).

About the Author

Alan Kraft has served as lead pastor of Christ Community Church (cccgreeley.org) in Greeley, Colorado, since 1990. He is passionate about teaching, writing, and prayer in order to help people experience Jesus in transformative ways. Alan and his wife, Raylene, love hanging out with their ever-growing family. He loves playing golf, reading William Kent Krueger novels, going on dates with his wife, and doing ministry with the amazing staff at Christ Community.

More information and resources regarding Alan's previous books or his teaching can be found at alankraft.com. Feel free to contact Alan at alank@cccgreeley.org for a conversation, a speaking opportunity, or a round of golf.

Printed in the USA
CPSIA information can be obtained
at www.ICGtesting.com
LVHW051103131223
766083LV00052B/1136